THE
FIERY
CUISINES

THE FIERY CUISINES

The World's Most Delicious Hot Dishes

DAVE DeWITT
and
NANCY GERLACH

ST. MARTIN'S PRESS
NEW YORK

Library of Congress Cataloging in Publication Data

DeWitt, Dave.
  The fiery cuisines.

  Includes index.
  1. Cookery, International.   2. Spices.   3. Condiments.
I. Gerlach, Nancy.   II. Title.
TX725.A1D475   1984   641.59   83-24545
ISBN 0-312-29211-2

Design by
Mina Greenstein

First Edition
10 9 8 7 6 5 4 3 2 1

Contents

Recipes

Appetizers

Salads

Soups

Sauces

Combination Entrees

Meat Dishes

Poultry Dishes

Seafood Dishes

Egg and Cheese Dishes

Pasta, Rice, and Potatoes

Vegetables

Breads

Part One
HOT
STUFF

1
A Nation Burns

In an intimate restaurant near the harbor in Nassau, British West Indies, two young tourists from Chicago are about to order lunch. A seemingly innocuous menu selection reads: "Conch Salad." It sounds good and looks even better—a small bowl of chopped seafood with onions and some green vegetable. The man raises the first modest spoonful to his lips and notices a wonderful aroma. Encouraged, he takes a bite. Immediately, a sensation unlike anything he has ever experienced spreads across his tongue, engulfs his mouth, and seems to cauterize his throat.

"Good grief, that's hot!" he says, tears streaming down his face. He is not sure if he should keep eating, but he's fascinated. The conch salad is terrifically hot, but it tastes great. His next timid sampling is easier to take; his mouth is either numb or adapting. By the time the bowl is empty, the man is perspiring, but proud. He's done it! He's finished the hottest food he's ever tasted. Little does he know that one bowl of conch meat with serrano chiles has changed his life. From that time on, his eating habits will never be the same. He's hooked on hot foods.

Scenes such as this are repeated every day as people discover a simple fact that aficionados have known for years—hot and spicy food can be delicious. And that discovery has led to an appreciation of fiery foods from all parts of the globe. It is our hope that this cookbook will both introduce newcomers to the delicious world of hot-food cooking and broaden the tastes of those who have come to love spicy dishes and are looking for the very best recipes.

Everyone knows at least one hot food lover. These are the asbestos-mouthed people who dare to order the "extra-hot" Szechuan dishes at their favorite Chinese restaurant, or liberally sprinkle Tabasco sauce on their scrambled eggs in the morning. They have learned that hot food cooking does not necessarily mean preparing dishes that only burn out your tonsils; rather, this is a cuisine that blends heat, fragrance, and flavor to produce spicy gourmet delicacies. In the past, particularly in America, truly hot ingredients were treated as condiments to be applied sparingly; there was no concept of entirely hot *meals*. But as more of us explore hot cuisines from around the world, the forecast is for a gourmet heat wave.

America's experimentation with fiery foods is a result of the importation of various hot ingredients, particularly chile peppers. The hotbeds of spicy cooking in America formed first in the southern states. In Louisiana, the introduction of a small, fiery red chile from the state of Tabasco, Mexico, transformed rice and seafood dishes into marvelously spicy concoctions. Jambalaya, the dish praised in song by Hank Williams, combines pork, ham, sausage, rice, and at least two kinds of chile heat—Tabasco and cayenne.

Cooks in North Carolina and Texas soon discovered that hot barbecue sauces, spread over smoked and charcoal-broiled meats, greatly enhanced the flavor of ribs, poultry, and steaks. These hot sauces depend on cayenne, Tabasco, or chile piquins for their pungency, though the more flavorful New Mexico red chiles are gaining ground as the principal ingredient for such sauces. Hot barbecue sauces are responsible for the popularity of Popeye's, a fried chicken franchise that features drumsticks and breasts marinated in Tabasco peppers. Hot barbecue restaurants such as Smoky's in New York have made a big success of spicy seasonings in the northern states.

Another great influence on hot-food cookery in the United States has been the corn cuisine of the state of Chihuahua in Mexico. The Sunbelt states of the American Southwest quickly adopted enchiladas and tamales, but that was just the beginning. As chile peppers increased in popularity in that region, cooks began experimenting with spicy foods as never before, for chile peppers are more than just a hot spice. They are the colorful red strings, or *ristras*, that decorate houses in the fall. They are the unique aroma of green chiles roasting over the grill to remove the skins. And they are complex, fascinating flavors like that of traditional Mexican *mole* sauce with its different varieties of chiles combined with chocolate and sesame seeds.

As Mexican influence spread over the Sunbelt states, Texans soon fashioned their own cuisine, called "Tex-Mex," which depends heavily upon the jalapeño chile and chile piquin for its blistering heat. This cooking is a combination of Mexican and Southern, based upon barbecuing and hot condiments. One dish in particular has evolved to represent Tex-Mex: chili con carne.

It is remarkable that one dish, chili con carne, should have hundreds of variations, but it is the subtle blend of several varieties of chiles and other spices that drives hot-food cooks to experiment. Most recipes for "true" chili con carne eliminate the beans, and the fragrance of pork simmering in a stew of onions, garlic, chiles, and cumin is truly unforgettable. In fact, there are heated debates in Texas and the rest of the Southwest as to whether the concocting of chili is an art or a science. We vote for art, and have attempted to capture one version of a masterpiece in a chili con carne recipe of our own (p. 36).

There are at least three major chili cookoffs or festivals each year in this country, and dozens of minor ones. The Wick Fowler Memorial World Championship Cookoff in Terlingua, Texas, attracts six to eight thousand chili enthusiasts each year. Chili-hungry crowds in excess of thirty thousand flood into Tropico, California, and Hatch, New Mexico, to celebrate the "pungent pod," as chile is affectionately called. The Hatch Chile Festival is endorsed by the International Connoisseurs of Red and Green Chile, a nonprofit organization sponsored by New Mexico State University to promote chiles. The Connoisseurs boast of over three thousand members in all fifty states and many foreign countries. Members include such notable fiery food fans as Ronald Reagan and Bob Hope.

One of the major reasons for such enthusiasm about hot

food dishes is the fact that they are exotic, yet easy to prepare. Our taste buds can travel to Africa for the piquant combination of peanuts and chiles; to Europe for complex tastes with mustards and horseradish; and to Sri Lanka for rice spiced with green chiles, ginger, and mustard seeds.

Admittedly, the burning sensation in our recipes is not for everybody, but it's not necessary to make the meals so scorching that they can't be tasted or appreciated. As we shall see, there are many possible heat levels and quite a number of hot ingredients that combine perfectly into fiery, yet delicious dishes.

2
Firepower: Where It Comes From

Of the more than four hundred spices in the world, the most pungent are the most popular. Although only chile truly scorches, there are a handful of others that approach the firepower of chile.

Black pepper, horseradish, ginger, mustard, and chiles all add excitement—and fire—to our food. All have varying degrees of heat when used alone or in combination for cooking, and at the end of this chapter you'll find a heat scale to gauge the relative pungency of each recipe.

Here is a brief "history of heat."

The Pepper Trade

"Pepper," said Plato, "is small in quantity and great in virtue." It was beloved by the Greeks and was the spice favorite of ancient Rome. Peppercorns were the first oriental spice to reach Europe and were in such demand that they were used as currency for about two thousand years. Pepper soon became an expression of a man's fortune, and the wealthy kept large stores of pepper in their houses as proof of solvency. One way of saying that a man was poor was that he "lacked pepper."

The pepper capital of the United States became Salem, Massachusetts. That small town was the focal point of a re-exporting business in pepper that saw about eight million pounds of the spice pass through New England to other countries on clipper ships. Hundreds of fast schooners were built exclusively for the pepper trade, which greatly helped the economy of the colonies.

Black pepper is *not* related to chile "peppers," which were misnamed by Columbus. Black pepper is a climbing vine cultivated throughout the East Indies that can reach a length of over thirty feet. The fruit of this vine is the peppercorn, which resembles (but hardly tastes like) a mistletoe berry. The tiny fruits are picked when they are yellowish red, and then are immersed in boiling water for about ten minutes. This process turns them black, and then the peppercorns are dried in the sun. Some peppercorns are picked green and sold fresh. The odor of pepper is penetrating and aromatic, while the taste is bitter and spicy hot.

Today pepper is consumed in great quantities and is probably the most commonly used spice around the world. It is usually combined with other spices during cooking, although in a few famous recipes such as Steak aux Trois Poivres (p. 121), it is the principal pungent ingredient.

The Radish That's Really a Mustard

There has always been confusion between the regular radish and horseradish, yet the latter is not a radish at all—it's a root crop more closely related to mustard.

In classical times, horseradish was prized for its medicinal qualities. The Greek physician Dioscorides believed it improved eyesight and aided in relieving cramps. Pliny claimed horseradish dissolved gallstones, though medical science has yet to confirm his findings. The Romans viewed horseradish suspiciously because they thought it promoted belching (and we know how refined Roman banquets were!).

Horseradish is native to central Europe, where it was first collected in the wild, and later cultivated. Because of its pungency, originally its consumption was considered to be beneath noble tastes and suitable only for peasants. But after its culinary properties were properly recognized, it became the principal ingredient of sauces to be served with roasted meats (see p. 115). Chaucer described its effect with the admonition: "Woe to the cook whose sauce has no sting." Concentrated forms of horseradish can bring tears to the eyes.

There has never been much of a world trade in horseradish because it grows easily in temperate zones throughout the world. In fact, in some cool, moist areas it is regarded as a weed. Most commercial horseradish preparations consist of the grated root alone, perhaps combined with vinegar and salt, or of a creamy sauce with the root as the pungent ingredient. Dehydrated horseradish is readily available on the spice shelves of most supermarkets. Combined with a tomato base, it is also used in a number of barbecue and seafood sauces. Its close relative, *wasabi*, or Japanese horseradish, is used to spice up sashimi and sushi (p. 207).

Taste Gingerly

Ginger, another root crop that has invaded America, is considered to be a native of Southeast Asia, where it has been used since ancient times. It was transported to the Mediterranean area about A.D. 1, accompanied by rumors about its supposed powers to cure flatulence and colic. Again, the early users of hot spices tended to put medicine before cooking. Because of the high profits possible in trading the roots, ginger also became one of the most popular spices in the world. By the eleventh century, ginger was well known in England, especially for use in baking. A few hundred years later, the Spanish introduced ginger into the West Indies and Mexico.

Queen Elizabeth I supposedly invented the gingerbread man by insisting that little ginger cakes be fashioned into likenesses of her friends. The English brought it to the Americas, and ginger became part of the standard rations for American soldiers during the Revolutionary War. The English appreciation for the spice was sharpened when they realized it was one of the important ingredients of the curry sauces of colonial India.

Ginger has a pleasant, slightly biting taste that can shock the system, especially when a piece is stuck to the roof of the mouth. Fresh ginger root is an important ingredient of chutneys (see Chapter 10, The Indian Subcontinent, p. 152), and tender young roots are often candied.

Ginger roots are now grown all over the world. Jamaica supplies most of the peeled (white) ginger, India is the source of unpeeled (gray) ginger, and West Africa exports dried ginger roots. Fresh, raw ginger is primarily used in cooking and as a spicy complement to seafood dishes. The extracts, powders, and oleoresins from ginger are utilized extensively in baked goods, meat dishes, soft drinks, and ice cream. Used in the home, ground ginger flavors breads, sauces, curry dishes, confections, and pickles. In the dried and powdered form, it resembles our next hot spice, mustard.

The Hot Weed

Because the origins of mustard are lost in prehistory, some experts believe that Cro-Magnon man began its cultivation. But since mustard is so easy to grow, it's entirely possible that "cultivation" in this case meant merely scattering the seeds about and waiting. Mustard spreads so rapidly that the Hindus considered it a fertility symbol, so mustard probably began its culinary career as a weed.

Mustard seeds have been collected and used medicinally since ancient times. The Greek father of medicine, Hippocrates, first mentioned the efficacy of mustard seeds for treating colds. Since his time, hot mustard baths and plasters have been standard medicine for chest colds.

Mustard now grows wild across most of the western United States, and credit for the spread of the hot weed is given to the Spanish padres who accompanied the conquistadores. It seems that they marked their trail by scattering mustard seeds along the way. The following years they could find their way back by following the tall mustard plants. The legacy of the padres now produces weeds on the range for farmers and ranchers.

The most commonly eaten varieties of the hot weed are white mustard, black mustard, and the most powerful of all, Indian or Chinese mustard. In the United States and Europe, mustard is sold in three ways: as seeds, as a dry powder that is mixed with water, and as a paste or cream sauce that is blended with other spices, wine, and vinegar. Its most common application is to spice up meats and salads, and a good example of its use occurs in our recipe for Fondue Bourguignonne (p. 119).

The pungency of mustard is similar to that of horseradish, to which it is related. It doesn't burn so much as shock the senses, particularly the nasal passages. Mustard in any form will lose its pungency as a result of oxidation, so it must be kept tightly sealed.

The Fiery Fruit

Chile "peppers" are one of the earliest domesticated crops of the New World, so it is ironic that hot dishes derived from them took so long to be introduced into the United States. Most history books tell us that Christopher Columbus "discovered" chiles in the West Indies while searching for India, and that he brought back to Europe, according to historian Peter Martyr in 1493, "peppers more pungent than that from the Caucasus." Martyr, of course, is comparing chiles to black pepper from the Caucasus. Chiles are actually fruits (in the botanical sense of a ripened ovary of a flower, containing seeds) of plants of the Solanaceae family, which includes tomatoes and eggplants.

Chiles were first domesticated in Mexico about 7,000 B.C. There is little doubt that Columbus was the first person to introduce the fiery fruit to Europeans, but tradition holds that Spanish explorers reintroduced chiles to Mexico and the American Southwest during their conquests. This theory has been accepted for decades and smugly suggests that Europeans were more appreciative of hot foods than the primitive societies they were ravishing. However, there are many pre-Columbian chile recipes, and there is no evidence that the Spanish gave chiles to the Indians; it is much more likely that the Pueblo Indians acquired them through trade with the Toltecs of Mexico.

By 1650, the cultivation and gastronomic use of chiles had spread throughout Europe, Asia, and Africa, and the fiery fruits had been adopted into the cuisines of many countries of the world. As befitting their origin, they became most popular in tropical climates. Only the milder forms of chiles, like pimientos and paprika, were used in Europe, where the pungency in foods came from mustard, horseradish, or black pepper.

Outside the Americas, the hottest chiles have been culti-vated in China, Africa, and Southeast Asia. Our collection of recipes from those areas illustrates the spread of chiles and the diversity of chile cuisines around the world.

As the appreciation for hot foods gained popularity in this country, mostly due to the increased population of the American Sunbelt, the demand for chiles grew so large that imports from Mexico were insufficient. Following the Mexican War of 1848, seeds from a fiery chile grown in the state of Tabasco were imported to Louisiana and grown by a judge named Avery and a banker named McIlhenny. It was their dream to create a sauce from the Tabasco chile that could be served with meats, soups, and seafood. Thus came the invention of Tabasco sauce, which has been one of the great success stories in chile lore. Their secret was mashing the Tabasco chiles into a fine paste, aging this paste in oaken casks for three years, and then mixing it with vinegar before bottling. Today there are a number of sauces made from Tabasco and other chiles on the market. Pickapeppa, a Jamaican chile sauce, is marketed throughout the world, and there are dozens of brands from Mexico and the American Sunbelt.

Although Tabasco sauce supplied much of America's crav-ing for hot spices, cultivation of other varieties of chiles began around 1898 near Las Cruces, New Mexico. Today, chile ranks number two on the world market in terms of dollar value, second only to black pepper. More than fifty thousand tons of chile varieties are harvested each year in the United States, and this figure does not include the related, but nonpungent, bell peppers.

CHILE HEAT

Regardless of the form chiles take—whole, powdered, oil, or sauces—they range in heat from spicy hot to truly inedible. This range is dependent upon the amount of a chemical called *capsaicin*, which occurs in veins near the seeds of the chile. An alkaloid, capsaicin is incredibly powerful and stable. The pure form can be detected by human taste buds in a dilution of one part in *one million*. It is seemingly unaffected by cold or heat, retaining its original potency despite time, cooking, or freezing. Since it resists oxidation, its power is not diminished by air, as is mustard. The degree of heat found in various kinds of chiles is controlled by genes that modify the amount of capsaicin present, not by the physical size of the chile itself. Often, the smaller the chile, the hotter it is.

We know that chiles are hot, but do they heat you up? Should Eskimos be eating enchiladas? And why on earth do sane, normal people eat hot foods in hot weather? Well, the startling fact is that the consumption of hot chiles makes you *cooler!* The capsaicin in chiles dilates the blood vessels, which increases blood circulation, thus enabling the body to perspire more. This action throws off heat, since perspiration is the body's natural cooling system.

Because of the fiery nature of chile pods and powder, it is a good idea to wear gloves while handling chiles. When transferred to the eyes or other sensitive body areas, capsaicin can cause severe burning. If you should accidentally be burned by chiles, immediately flush the eyes with water and wash other areas with large amounts of soapy water.

There is a myth that suggests that one becomes "macho" in direct proportion to the degree of chile heat one can consume. Some men (and women) indulge in jalapeño-eating contests, risking stomach injuries to prove their pungency prowess. Actually, the ability to withstand capsaicin is not related to gender or hormones; it is simply a matter of bodily acclimatization. One seems to build up a tolerance to chile heat gradually, until the tears finally disappear.

A bit of advice: When eating food that is too hot, most people yelp and chug a glass of water. But capsaicin is insoluble in water; like oil and water, they don't mix. Water-based liquids such as beer or soda actually force the capsaicin into your stomach, displacing it but not neutralizing it. Dairy products, on the other hand, do neutralize capsaicin to a certain degree. So reach for yoghurt, sour cream, or milk if you've eaten food that is too fiery.

THE SCOVILLE SCALE

There is quite a bit of confusion about measuring the relative heat of spicy ingredients because chemical tests do not consider individual reactions, which differ according to acclimatization. As it turns out, all pungency measurements are subjective. In 1919, a pharmacologist named Scoville devised a method to test for relative heat that is still used today. A measured weight of chiles is processed to extract the capsaicin, and then dilutions are made for testing. A panel of five "heat experts" is convened for the "torture test," and they proceed to taste and evaluate the dilutions for relative heat. The pungency is recorded in multiples of one hundred "Scoville units." A majority of three members of the panel must agree before a rating is assigned and although there is an attempt to be scientific and objective, a Scoville panel resembles a wine-tasting party more than a careful lab test. We hope that this collection of recipes will inspire hot food lovers to convene their own Scoville test groups.

On the Scoville scale, very mild heat rates about 100 units, while extremely hot chiles score over 10,000 units. We have attempted to construct a pungency rating for each recipe in this book by using the following table. Note that our heat scale is exponential, and thus a rating of eight is not twice as hot as four, but rather *four times* as hot. And please remember that any heat rating is subjective and approximate. *The rating of ten is theoretical and applies only to the very hottest chiles in pure form, not prepared meals.*

Heat Scale Rating	Hot Ingredients	Approximate Scoville Units
10	Legendary chiles—"Bahama Mama" and "Texas Fireball"	20,000 +
9	Santaka (Japanese varieties)	15,000
8	Tabasco, chile piquins, celestials, other small chiles	12,000
7	Jalapeños, serranos, chile oil	10,000
6	Chipotle chiles, "chili powder"	8,000
5	Sandia chiles, Mexican hot sauces	5,000
4	Pasilla, Rio Grande, Fresno, black, and ancho chiles	3,000
3	NuMex Big Jim chiles, yellow (wax) chiles, curry powder	1,500
2	Anaheim chiles, black pepper, Chinese mustard, NuMex R-Naky chiles	500
1	Ginger, horseradish, other mustards, cherry and tomato peppers, paprika, pimiento	100–200

3
Pungent
Preparations

Hot ingredients are readily available in some form in most cities in the United States. However, since it may be difficult to find, say, fresh green chiles or horseradish in certain areas or all year round, we have prepared a comprehensive list of pungent preparations, including substitutions, in order to make it easier to prepare certain hot recipes in this book.

PEPPER

There are three kinds of pepper available on the market, which in reality are three variants of the same peppercorn. Green peppercorns are picked fresh, then pickled and bottled. Often they are mashed before adding to recipes. Dried black peppercorns are used whole, crushed, or powdered. In powdered form they become common pepper for use in shakers—a mixture of black and white. White pepper is the ground core of the peppercorn with the black hull removed. It is used in recipes where black pepper would discolor the food, as in white sauces. White pepper is less pungent than black pepper or whole peppercorns. Recently some more exotic varieties of peppercorns such as Szechuan have come on the market, but they are not much more pungent than the familiar black peppercorn.

HORSERADISH

In many parts of the country horseradish root is available fresh. It should be peeled and then grated. Other forms include the dehydrated powder, which can be reconstituted by mixing it with a little water, and bottled horseradish, which retains its pungency fairly well.

GINGER

Ginger is available as the fresh root in all parts of this country. The root should be peeled and then sliced or grated. Powdered ginger is utilized in baking and in sauce recipes. Imported crystallized ginger is also available, but is considered more of a candy than a cooking ingredient.

MUSTARD

The three basic forms of mustard available to the consumer are seeds, powder, and prepared (bottled) varieties. All vary to a certain degree in spiciness, with the black or Chinese mustard taking the pungency prize. Prepared mustards are a combination of mustard powder and other ingredients, usually spices and vinegar. The finest and most pungent prepared mustards are the French or Dijon-style. Prepared mustard may be substituted for powder in most recipes.

FRESH OR GREEN CHILES

These are mostly available from July through October in the southwestern United States, although they are appearing with more frequency these days in other areas. Usually the green chiles are either the mild Anaheim and Big Jim varieties or the hotter New Mexico cultivars such as #6-4, Sandia, and Rio Grande. It is very difficult to gauge the relative heat of these large chiles, but a standard rule of thumb is the larger the chile, the milder it is. All of the green chile varieties have a tough skin that must be removed before using. Slit the chiles first, roast them in the oven or over a charcoal fire until the skin begins to blister and separate, then plunge the chiles in cold water and peel them. Be sure to wear gloves during the peeling and to remove the stem and seeds. Fresh red chiles, which are just more ripened, are handled in the same way. In recipes, you may substitute canned green chile or frozen green chiles for the fresh ones. In some cases jalapeños or other smaller chiles may be used instead, but the taste will not be the same and the heat will be much greater.

Chiles are very high in vitamins C and A. In fact, gram for gram fresh chiles have more vitamin C than a Valencia orange. Dried red chile has almost twice the amount of vitamin A as a carrot. They retain these vitamins despite cooking, but drying chiles will drastically reduce the vitamin C concentration.

DRIED RED OR BLACK CHILE PODS

Packaged in various-sized plastic bags, these pods are generally pureed to make chile sauces or ground into powder. They keep for quite a while, but be sure to keep them dry to avoid molding. The chile varities used are generally the hotter ones, and the Mexican varieties include ancho, pasilla, and chile negro. Ground chile powder may be substituted for pods in most recipes, but be careful when using cayenne powder because it is usually much hotter.

CHILE POWDERS AND FLAKES

"Chili powder" in bottles is most often a blend of medium-hot ground pods, plus spices like cumin, oregano, and garlic. It can be used as a garnish or in quantity for chile sauces if pods or plain ground chile is not available. Southwestern markets and some mail-order houses sell ground chile by variety or by degree of heat without any other spices added. Cayenne powder, as mentioned above, is extremely hot and should be used with caution. Chile flakes are broken pieces of smaller hot chiles and generally have more heat than flavor. Paprika is a very mild chile that is ground into a powder and used as a condiment and a base for certain sauces. Some varieties of packaged paprika have more heat than others; to spice up mild paprika, mix it with cayenne or other ground chiles.

BOTTLED CHILE SAUCES

There are a bewildering number of domestic and imported sauces that contain some variety of chile. They are generally used as a garnish, a base for a dip or other sauce, or as a principal heat source in some recipes. Tabasco sauce is probably the most famous, and it is quite hot. Mexican sauces are found on both sides of the border and are usually of medium heat and quite tasty. Some milder chile sauces are made in the Carribean and consist of chiles plus fruit extracts such as mango. Pickapeppa, which is made in Jamaica, is an excellent sauce for meats and seafood. Another Caribbean specialty is sherry pepper sauce, which can be made at home by steeping santaka chiles in sherry. Sherry pepper sauces are commonly used with seafood or added to drinks like Bloody Marys. From the Orient come the hottest sauces of all, which are actually chile oils. Santakas or chile piquins are steeped in peanut oil for weeks to make a sauce for use in cooking meat and seafood.

CURRY POWDERS

Curried dishes are usually seasoned according to individual recipes rather than with a general powder, as the Indians believe that poultry should be seasoned differently than fish. But for most hot recipes contained in this book, a commercially prepared curry powder such as Madras is perfectly acceptable. To spice up a mild curry powder, add some cayenne. Below is a formula for a basic curry powder that can be made at home.

> 5 tablespoons hot dried red chile powder
> $1/2$ teaspoon powdered ginger
> $1/2$ teaspoon mustard seeds
> $1/2$ tablespoon cloves
> 2 inch stick of cinnamon
> 4 tablespoons coriander seeds
> 4 tablespoons cumin seeds
> 3 tablespoons turmeric
> $1/2$ teaspoon fenugreek
> $1/2$ teaspoon cardamom

Mix all the ingredients together and grind in a blender until fine.

Mail-Order Sources

Often, hot ingredients are difficult to find at the neighborhood supermarket. Inquire from the firms below about their pungent products.

Casados Farms
P.O. Box 852
San Juan Pueblo, NM 87566
(selection of dried New
Mexico chiles)

Horticultural Enterprises
P.O. Box 34082
Dallas, TX 75234
(seeds for many varieties of
chiles)

Williams Sonoma
P.O. Box 7456
San Francisco, CA 94120
(many fine mustards)

Tia Mia, Inc.
Sunland Park, NM 88063
(canned, dried chiles;
canned sauces)

Paprikas Weiss
1546 Second Avenue
New York, NY 10028
(imported Hungarian
paprika)

Moneo and Sons
210 W. 14th St.
New York, NY 10011
(Mexican and Latin
specialties)

How The Recipes Are Organized

The recipes in this book are arranged according to region first to present an overview of the distribution and variation of hot foods worldwide. Within each regional chapter, the recipes are organized in the following order:

Appetizers/Hors d'Oeuvres
Salads
Soups
Salsas/Relishes/Accompaniments
Combination Entrées

Meats: beef, pork, veal, lamb, goat, game
Poultry: chicken, turkey, duck, game hen
Seafood: shellfish, fish, frog
Cheese
Egg
Starches: beans, rice, potatoes
Vegetables
Special Dishes

Within each recipe, the ingredients are listed in the order in which they appear in the instructions, with the exception of the hot ingredients, which always appear first. This arrangement is intended to give the curious (or wary) cook a quick glimpse at the pungent properties of the dish. Also included with each recipe is a heat scale indication keyed to the standards found in Chapter 2, Firepower. In an attempt to give the cook as much latitude as possible, we have included some serving suggestions and variations.

You'll be happy to know that the recipes in this book have been selected as much for flavor as heat. It's easy to increase the heat in any recipe, so the point is not to make the dishes unbearably hot. The tastiest spicy dishes are those naturally delicious ones that are enhanced by just the right amount of spice to make them truly tasty hot foods. It is important that you know the "fire power" of the ingredients you are using, especially when dealing with chiles or chile powder. Green chiles vary in intensity by variety; crushed red chile can range from nearly sweet to hot, and crushed piquins and santakas should be approached with caution and respect. As a result, a particular recipe can vary from mild up to untouchable depending on both the quality as well as the quantity of the fiery ingredients. So if in doubt about the power of your ingredients, start with a small amount and add until the desired heat is attained; remember that it is a simple matter to add more "fire" to any recipe.

Part Two
RECIPES

4
The American Sunbelt

The term "Sunbelt" in this chapter refers to the southern and southwestern states of the United States that were the areas originally influenced by the hot cuisines of other areas. In Texas, New Mexico, Arizona, and California, the hot chile sauces served with corn dishes originated in the Mexican state of Chihuahua. Now considered food suitable for international gourmets, such "Mexican" cooking was originally the food of the peasants, as was much of the fiery cuisine found in the recipes to follow.

Because of the regional adaptations of chile sauces and other hot ingredients used in the Sunbelt, the term "Mexican cooking" is no longer accurate. Cooking in California is far milder than in New Mexico; Texans prefer jalapeños to green chile and Arizona chile cookery tends to be sweeter than that of other states. The pungency of the chiles used varies enormously, especially outside the Sunbelt. Experimentation and tasting are the only ways to be certain you do not burn your guests.

A collision of cultures in Louisiana and adjacent states produced a hot cuisine that looks to Tabascos and cayenne chiles for its heat. The French colonists (Creoles), French-Canadians (Cajuns), and freed African slaves all contributed to dishes in which the heat is usually added after the meal is served, more as condiments than food. Chiles are utilized in sauces over seafood and cayenne powder is added as others would use salt and pepper.

25

Since it is obvious that heat can be added to any food after cooking with sauces or powders, we have included only those Creole or Cajun recipes in which the hot ingredients are used during cooking.

There must be hundreds of recipes for barbecue sauces and dishes, which originated in the American South and West. Included here are some of the best. Remember that the relative heat can be easily adjusted.

Chile con Queso
(NEW MEXICO)

This chile and cheese dish is excellent as a party dip and can also be "recycled" as a hot cheese sauce with baked potatoes or over vegetables.

4–5 green chiles, skinned, seeds removed, chopped
1 onion, chopped fine
3 tablespoons oil or shortening
2 tablespoons flour
2 cups milk
1/4 cup water
2 tomatoes, peeled and chopped
1 pound cheddar cheese, grated

Sauté the onion in the shortening until soft. Stir in the flour and heat for 2 minutes.

Combine the milk and water and stir into the flour mixture and heat until slightly thickened. Add the tomatoes, chiles, and cheese. Stir over medium heat until the cheese has melted.

Yield: 3 cups
Serving Suggestions: Serve warm in a chafing dish with tostadas or corn chips. Put the chips in small bowls and ladle the hot cheese sauce over them.
HEAT SCALE: 4

Cream Cheese Chile Dip

(NEW MEXICO)

Although called a dip, this cream cheese spread can also be used as a stuffing for celery sticks and on crackers or bread as a Southwestern canapé.

3 green chiles, skinned, seeds removed, chopped fine
1 8-ounce package cream cheese
2 tablespoons milk
1 tablespoon onion, minced
Pinch of garlic salt

Combine all the ingredients and beat until creamy, adding more milk if necessary. Allow the dip to sit for an hour or more before serving, to blend the flavors.

Yield: 1 cup
Serving Suggestions: Serve as an appetizer with chips or raw vegetables.
HEAT SCALE: 4

Creole Cocktail Sauce

(LOUISIANA)

In Louisiana, this spicy sauce is a favorite with both shrimp and oysters.

2–3 tablespoons fresh horseradish, peeled and minced
2 teaspoons Tabasco sauce
1 cup catsup
Juice of ¹/₂ lemon or lime
Salt to taste

Combine all ingredients and puree until smooth. Let this mixture sit refrigerated for at least one hour to blend all ingredients.

Yield: 1–1¼ cups
Serving Suggestions: Pour the sauce into cocktail glasses. Arrange cooked and shelled shrimp on the rims of the glasses, garnish the sauce with 1 grated hard-cooked egg, and serve with lemon wedges.
HEAT SCALE: 3

Chile Salad Dressing
(NEW MEXICO)

This is New Mexico's answer to "Green Goddess" dressing.

2–3 fresh green chiles, skinned, seeds removed, chopped fine,
*   or 3 serranos, chopped fine*
1 clove garlic, minced
1 medium onion, chopped
¼ cup water
3 medium avocados, mashed
Juice of 2 lemons or limes
Pinch each of oregano, basil, and thyme
¾ cup salad oil

Puree the chiles, garlic, and onion in the water. Add the mashed avocado, lemon or lime juice, and seasonings and mix well. Slowly add the oil until the desired consistency is obtained.

Yield: 2 to 3 cups
Serving Suggestions: This dressing goes well with any crisp garden salad but is especially good with sliced tomatoes, garnished with parsley or fresh cilantro.
Variation: Add ½ cup sour cream for a creamier dressing.
HEAT SCALE: 3

Salsa Fria

(NEW MEXICO)

Salsa fria, or "cold sauce" because it isn't cooked, is an all-purpose sauce that can be set on the table for general use. Although most commonly served with chips as an appetizer, salsa fria can be used as an accompaniment to beef tacos or other Mexican foods. The keys to the sauce are the fresh cilantro and very finely chopped ingredients. Adjust the degree of heat by the number and type of chiles used. This salsa is modeled after the recipe served at the La Florida Bar in Juarez, Mexico.

4–6 jalapeño or serrano chiles, chopped very fine (fresh,
    frozen, or canned green chile may be substituted)
2 large onions, chopped very fine
2 large ripe tomatoes, peeled and chopped very fine
3 cloves garlic, chopped very fine
2 small bunches fresh cilantro, minced
1/4 cup red wine vinegar
1/4 cup oil
1/4 teaspoon oregano
1/2 teaspoon salt (optional)

Mix all ingredients together in a bowl and refrigerate for at least one hour before serving.

Yield: 2 cups
Serving Suggestions: With chips, this salsa makes a perfect dip for an appetizer before a huge Mexican dinner.
HEAT SCALE: 5

Salsa de Chile Verde

Basic Green Chile Sauce

(NEW MEXICO)

Most cooked chile sauces served in Mexico are made with dried red chile pods. This green sauce is more commonly found in the American Southwest, particularly in New Mexico, where the recipe originated.

5–6 fresh green chiles, skinned, seeds removed, chopped
1 large onion, chopped
2 cloves garlic, chopped fine
2 tablespoons oil
1 large tomato, peeled and chopped (optional)
1/2 teaspoon cumin powder (optional)
1/2 teaspoon coriander powder (optional)
1 1/2 cups water
Salt to taste

Sauté the onion and garlic in the oil until transparent, add the remaining ingredients, and simmer for 30 minutes.

Yield: 2 cups
Serving Suggestions: This versatile sauce can be used with enchiladas, tacos, tostados, as a dip, or to accompany beef, chicken, or fish.
Variations: Puree in a blender for a smoother sauce. Eliminate the tomato for a "purist's" sauce. Add 1 or 2 ground santaka chiles for a hotter sauce.
HEAT SCALE: 6

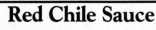

Red Chile Sauce

(NEW MEXICO)

Make this basic sauce from fresh, frozen, or dried red chiles, or, if you prefer, chile powder may be used. Do not make it with cayenne powder if you value your life. Remove the skins and seeds of the fresh red chiles before using. Remove the seeds and stems from dried pods. Dried Mexican pods such as pasilla, chile negro, or ancho may be substituted.

5 red chile pods or the equivalent
1 cup water
2 cloves garlic, chopped
2 tablespoons oil
1 medium onion, chopped
1/2 teaspoon cumin powder
1/2 teaspoon coriander powder
Salt to taste

Tear the chile pods into strips and soak them in 1 cup hot water for 20 minutes. Puree the chile and water in a blender until smooth. Add all the remaining ingredients and simmer for 1 hour.

Remove the coarse sauce from the heat and blend it again for a smooth sauce.

Yield: About 2 cups
Serving Suggestions: Use this sauce with enchiladas, tacos, tamales, as a dip, or as an accompaniment to meat and poultry dishes.
Variation: 1 or 2 santaka or piquin chiles may be added for extra heat.
HEAT SCALE: 5

Barbecue Sauce

(NEW MEXICO)

Chile and mustard are combined in this sauce with a bite. Spicy barbecue sauce first originated in the South as Tabasco sauce added to a tomato-based sauce—but this one is definitely a Southwestern invention.

4 dried red chiles, crumbled
4 chile piquins
1/4 cup prepared chile sauce
1 teaspoon dry mustard
1 cup hot water
1 medium onion, chopped
1 clove garlic, minced
1 tablespoon bacon drippings
1/2 cup catsup
2 1/2 tablespoons vinegar
2 tablespoons brown sugar
1 teaspoon Worcestershire sauce
1 teaspoon Liquid Smoke

Soak the chiles in the hot water for 15 minutes. Sauté the onion and garlic in the drippings until soft. Add the remaining ingredients and simmer for 2 hours. Puree the mixture in a blender until smooth.

Yield: 2 cups
Serving Suggestions: This sauce goes well with chicken, beef, or pork. It is especially good when used to baste grilled meats.
Variation: For a milder sauce, leave out the chile piquins.
Note: This recipe requires advance preparation.
HEAT SCALE: 6

Creole Jambalaya

Most recipes for this dish de-emphasize the hot ingredients, but our informants in Louisiana insist that Tabasco and cayenne are essential in this Spanish-Creole favorite. And the Creoles are known for seasoning liberally with cayenne!

1/4 teaspoon cayenne powder
2 teaspoons Tabasco sauce
3 tablespoons butter
1 pound pork in 1/2-inch cubes
2 large onions, minced
1 cup cooked ham in 1/2-inch cubes
5 cloves garlic, minced
1 teaspoon thyme
2 bay leaves
1 tablespoon fresh parsley, minced
1/2 teaspoon ground cloves
1/2 pound Italian sausage
3 cups hot beef broth
1 1/2 cups rice

Melt the butter in a saucepan and add the pork and onion. Sauté until the onion is soft and the pork is lightly browned. Add the ham, garlic, thyme, bay leaves, parsley, and cloves and sauté for an additional 5 minutes. Coarsely chop the sausage, add to the pork mixture, and sauté for 5 minutes. Then add the broth and bring to a boil, reduce heat, and simmer for 10 minutes.

Add the rice, cayenne, and Tabasco and bring again to a boil. Then reduce the heat and cook for about 20 minutes, stirring occasionally until the rice is cooked and the broth has been absorbed.

Serves: 6 to 8
Serving Suggestions: This is a meal in itself, but a green salad and French bread turn this meal into a feast.
HEAT SCALE: 4

Posole

(NEW MEXICO)

Christmas in New Mexico would not be the same without a bowl of traditional posole, though this dish is popular all year long. It is an easy to prepare "stew" that can be done in a crock pot. There are many variations of posole—we have included our favorite.

6 tablespoons ground red chile
2 cups posole corn* (substitute hominy if posole is not available)
2 pounds pork, diced
1 onion, chopped
2 cloves garlic, minced
2 teaspoons dried oregano, crushed (optional)
1 teaspoon vinegar
Salt to taste

Cover the posole with water and simmer until the kernels "pop."
    Add the remaining ingredients and bring to a boil. Reduce the heat, cover, and simmer until the pork is very tender and begins to fall apart. Add more water if necessary.

Serves: 6
HEAT SCALE: 6

Chile Verde con Carne

Green Chile Stew
(NEW MEXICO)

This is a staple dish in New Mexico—no cold winter Sunday would be complete without a football game and a bowl of green

*Posole is a lime-dried corn.

chile. There are many variations of this dish, so experiment with your own ideas.

6–8 green chiles, skinned, seeds removed, chopped (or more for
    heat)
2 pounds stew meat (pork preferred or substitute beef), cut into
    1-inch cubes
2 tablespoons oil
2 large onions, chopped
1 clove garlic, chopped
1 quart water
2 large tomatoes, peeled and chopped
2 large potatoes, chopped (optional)
1/4 teaspoon cumin (optional)
Salt to taste

Brown the meat in oil, add the onion and garlic, and sauté for 10 minutes. Put the water and all the other ingredients in a kettle or crock pot, add the meat, onion and garlic, and cook for 2 or more hours or until the meat is very tender and starts to fall apart.

Serves: 6

Serving Suggestions: Green chile stew can be served as a main dish or as the basis of a number of other recipes (see below).

Variations: An old El Paso favorite is *caldillo*, a dish very similar to the above recipe except that round steak is used as the meat. Potatoes are common in *caldillo* and occasionally jalapeños are substituted for green chiles. Leftover chile stew can be turned into a delicious casserole by lining a baking dish with biscuit dough, pouring in the stew, and topping it with grated cheddar cheese. Bake for 45 minutes in a 350°F oven.

HEAT SCALE: 6

Chile con Carne

(TEXAS)

There are probably a million recipes for this immensely popular dish, and a half-dozen cookbooks specializing in the variations. Although many purists consider the addition of beans to be an adulteration, we advise you to go with your own taste.

7 dried red chiles, seeds removed, crumbled
2 pounds chuck, cut into ¹/₂-inch cubes or coarsely ground
2 tablespoons oil
1 large onion, chopped
1 clove garlic, chopped
3 cups water
3 tomatoes, peeled and chopped (optional)
¹/₂ teaspoon dried oregano
¹/₄ teaspoon basil
¹/₄ teaspoon cumin (optional)
2 cups cooked kidney or pinto beans (optional)
Salt to taste

Brown the meat in the oil, add the onion and garlic, and sauté until the onion is soft.

Blend the chiles in 1 cup of the water. Add the chile mixture and the remaining water to the meat and simmer for 1 hour. Add all the other ingredients, except the beans, and simmer for another hour. Add more water if necessary.

Add the beans and cook until the mixture is thick, about 15 to 30 minutes.

Serves: 6
Serving Suggestions: Corn bread and coleslaw go well with this Southwestern stew.
HEAT SCALE: 6

Red Chile con Carne
(NEW MEXICO)

This is a New Mexican version of the dish, which means beans are *never* used. It is easy to prepare and the flavor of the chile improves if prepared a day in advance of serving.

6–8 dried red chiles
3 cups water
2 pounds pork, cut in cubes
2 tablespoons oil
3 cloves garlic
Salt to taste

Heat 1 cup of the water to boiling, then pour it over the chiles and let them steep for 15 minutes.

Fry the pork in the oil until lightly browned. Pour off the excess fat.

Puree the chiles and garlic in the water the chiles were steeped in until smooth.

Add the chile mixture and the remaining water to the pork. Bring to a boil, then reduce the heat and simmer until the pork is very tender and starts to fall apart, at least 2 hours.

Serves: 6 to 8
HEAT SCALE: 7

Chile and Onion Pie

(ARIZONA)

This Sunbelt "quiche" makes an excellent luncheon dish.

PIE SHELL
1 cup flour
1/2 teaspoon salt
1/2 teaspoon lemon rind, grated
6 tablespoons butter
3 tablespoon chilled white tequila

Sift the flour and salt and add the lemon rind. Cut the butter into pieces and, using your fingertips, rub it into the flour mixture until it looks like coarse cornmeal. Use the chilled tequila to work the dough until it holds together.

On a lightly floured surface, roll out the dough until it is large enough to fit a 10-inch pie pan. Place the dough in the pan and shape it to fit firmly and trim the excess dough. Line the shell with buttered aluminum foil and hold it in place with dried beans, rice, or rock salt.

Bake the shell in a 350°F oven for 15 minutes. Remove the foil and beans, prick the shell all over with a fork, and return the shell to the oven and bake uncovered for an additional 10 to 15 minutes or until golden brown.

PIE FILLING
1/2 cup green chiles, skinned, seeds removed, chopped
Dash chile powder
1/3 cup butter, melted
2 tablespoons dried bread crumbs
1/2 cup Parmesan cheese, freshly grated
2 green onions, chopped, including the greens
4 eggs
2 egg yolks

¹/₄ teaspoon cayenne pepper
1 teaspoon dry mustard
1 teaspoon prepared mustard (Dijon preferred)
Salt to taste
2¹/₂ cups milk, scalded
1 tablespoon white tequilla

Place the browned pastry shell on a baking sheet for support and brush the bottom of the shell with 1 tablespoon of the melted butter. Combine the bread crumbs and 2 tablespoons of the Parmesan cheese and sprinkle the mixture over the bottom of the shell.

Sauté the green onions in 2 tablespoons of the butter until soft, then set aside.

Combine the eggs and egg yolks and whisk until thick. Stir in the two mustards, salt, and cayenne and blend well. Stir the remaining cooled melted butter into the mixture. Mix ¹/₄ cup of the Parmesan cheese and the scalded milk and stir into the egg mixture. Add the green chiles, tequila, and cooked green onions. Mix well and pour into the pastry shell.

Bake for 30 to 40 minutes in a 350°F oven or until the filling sets. Remove from the oven, top with the remaining Parmesan cheese, sprinkle with the chile powder, and serve.

Serves: 6 to 8
HEAT SCALE: 5

Tamale Pie with Cheese and Chicken

(NEW MEXICO)

By varying the accompaniments, this casserole can be served as a luncheon entrée as well as a hearty dinner. It has the basics of tamales but is much easier to prepare.

4 green chiles, skinned, seeds removed, chopped
2 jalapeños, minced
1 teaspoon red chile powder
1 4-pound chicken
2 large onions, sliced and separated into rings
2 cloves garlic, minced
1 teaspoon dried basil, crushed
2 whole cloves
1 bay leaf
1 cup ripe olives, chopped
1 cup whole kernel corn
2 cups sour cream
Salt to taste

Boil the chicken, half the onion, garlic, basil, cloves, and bay leaf in water to cover until the chicken starts to fall away from the bone. Remove the chicken, strain the broth, and reserve.

Remove the meat from the bone and chop the chicken and remaining onion. Combine with the remaining ingredients, except broth. Place in a casserole dish and cover with the following topping:

TOPPING

2 cups chicken broth (from above)
1 cup masa harina (corn flour, not meal)
2 eggs, separated
2 cups Monterey Jack cheese, grated

Bring the broth to a boil and gradually add the masa while stirring constantly. Reduce the heat and cook until the mixture thickens, about 10 minutes. Remove from heat and stir in the egg yolks. Whip the egg whites until stiff and fold them into the masa mixture. Spread this batter over the casserole and top with the grated cheese.

Bake for 35 minutes at 375°F.

Serves: 6
Serving Suggestions: An avocado and grapefruit salad goes well with this "pie." Serve with a green vegetable such as peas, green beans, or zucchini.

HEAT SCALE: 4

Chicken Chimichangas

(ARIZONA)

Here is a very popular dish from Arizona. How and where it originated is a mystery; the word "chimichanga" has no English translation—it may as well be called "thing-a-ma-jig." Basically, a chimichanga is a deep-fried burrito.

3–4 green chiles, skinned, seeds removed, chopped
1/2 cup onion, chopped
2 tablespoons butter
2 cups cooked chicken, shredded
1/2 cup sour cream
1/2 cup cheddar cheese, grated
1/4 cup black olives, chopped
4 flour tortillas

Sauté the onion in butter until soft, then combine all the ingredients for the filling.

Place 1/2 cup of filling in the middle of each large flour tortilla; fold up the top and bottom and sides. Secure with toothpicks if necessary.

Deep-fry in hot oil, turning constantly, until browned all over.

Serves: 4

Serving Suggestions: Cover each chimichanga with guacamole or sour cream and serve with refried beans and rice.

Variations: Almost any type of filling can be used. Substitute beef, pork, or refried beans for the chicken. Green or red chile stew can also be used.

HEAT SCALE: 4

Fajitas

(TEXAS)

Texans love to barbecue and are quite inventive when it comes to outdoor cooking, as evidenced by the following recipe.

¹/2 cup canned jalapeños, chopped fine
¹/3 cup jalapeño juice (from canned jalapeños)
¹/3 cup soy sauce
¹/3 cup port wine
2 pounds flank or skirt steak
8 flour tortillas
Salsa borracha (see p. 55)

Combine the soy sauce, jalapeño juice, and wine. Trim and score the meat and marinate in the sauce for 24 hours.

Grill the steak over charcoal until done and carve diagonally against the grain in thin strips as for London broil.

To serve, place pieces of steak in a flour tortilla, cover with the chopped jalapeños, and eat like a sandwich.

Serves: 8

Note: This recipe requires advance preparation.

HEAT SCALE: 6

Pork Ribs—Texan Style

Ginger and small hot chiles are bases for the pungency of the sweet and sour ribs. These can be grilled outdoors or under a broiler.

6 chile piquins (or more, to taste), crushed
2 teaspoons fresh ginger, peeled and minced
4 pounds pork spareribs in racks
4 cloves garlic, whole
1 tablespoon cornstarch mixed with 1 tablespoon water
1 cup pineapple juice
2 tablespoons soy sauce
2 tablespoons vinegar
1 teaspoon cumin powder
10 pineapple rings (fresh preferred)

Rub the ribs vigorously with the garlic and set aside.

Combine the cornstarch, pineapple juice, soy sauce, vinegar, cumin, piquins, and ginger in a pan. Slowly bring to a boil, reduce the heat, and simmer until the sauce is thick, stirring constantly.

Place the ribs on a grill or under a broiler. Baste the exposed side with the sauce, and baste again in 5 minutes. After 10 minutes, turn the ribs and baste the second side and cook 10 minutes more.

If you are using a broiler, place the pineapple rings on the ribs and baste both the rings and ribs with the sauce and cook for about 15 minutes.

If you are cooking over coals, turn the ribs a second time, place the pineapple rings on top and baste a final time. Cook for about 10 minutes more.

Serves: 6 to 8
Serving Suggestions: Delicious with roasted corn on the cob and potato salad.
HEAT SCALE: 4

Carne Adovada

(NEW MEXICO)

This recipe has been prepared in New Mexico for hundreds of years. Before the advent of refrigeration, it was a convenient way to preserve pork, as the chile acts as an antioxidant to retard spoilage. Traditional carne adovada is extremely hot.

8 ounces dried red chile, coarsely crumbled
3 cups water
4 cloves garlic, minced
2 pounds pork, cut in 2-inch strips

Pour 1 cup of hot water over the chiles and let stand for 20 minutes. Put the chiles, garlic, and remaining water in a blender and puree.

Cover the pork strips with the chile sauce and marinate for 24 hours in the refrigerator.

Bake the pork in the marinade for 3 hours in a 300°F oven.

Serves: 6.

Serving Suggestions: Carne adovada is served like a stew in a shallow bowl accompanied by flour tortillas.

Variation: Before baking, add 2 or 3 diced potatoes and a chopped onion.

Note: This recipe requires advance preparation.

HEAT SCALE: 8

Chile Rellenos

(NEW MEXICO)

Here is a classic chile dish, stuffed whole chiles. Properly prepared, they are incredibly delicious.

8 whole green chiles, fresh or canned, skinned, seeds removed
Monterey Jack or cheddar cheese, cut into sticks
Flour for dredging
4 eggs, separated
4 tablespoons flour
2 teaspoons baking powder
1 tablespoon water
1/4 teaspoon salt

Cut a slit in each chile and stuff with cheese sticks. Pat dry and set aside.

Beat the egg whites until stiff. Combine the remaining ingredients and gently fold them into the egg whites to make a batter.

Roll the stuffed chiles in flour and carefully dip them into the batter and coat well. Deep-fry the chiles, turning them constantly until lightly browned. Remove and drain.

Serves: 4
Serving Suggestions: Top with a chile sauce (either red or green) and serve the traditional accompaniments, rice and beans.
Variations: Chiles can be stuffed with a variety of fillings including picadillo (p. 79), ground meats plus cheese, or refried beans. For a chile relleno casserole, line a baking dish with the stuffed chiles, pour the batter over the top, and bake 40 minutes in a 350°F oven. Pour your choice of sauce over the top before serving.
HEAT SCALE: 3

Potatoes with Red Chile

(NEW MEXICO)

These are Southwestern hash browns with a "bite."

1 tablespoon red chile powder
3 tablespoons oil or bacon fat
Salt to taste
2 cups potatoes, diced
1 small onion, diced

Heat the oil and several pinches of salt in a frying pan, then add the potatoes and fry until tender. Remove the potatoes, add the onion and chile powder to the oil, and sauté.

Add the potatoes and fry until the potatoes are well browned.

Serves: 4
Serving Suggestions: Goes very well with huevos rancheros (see p. 66); adds color and heat to a grilled steak dinner with corn or peas.
HEAT SCALE: 3

Green Rice

(NEW MEXICO)

Here is a New World pilaf variation that is very versatile and simple to prepare. It probably originated in Mexico after rice became a staple there and was later introduced into the American Southwest.

4 green chiles, skinned, seeds removed, chopped
2 cups long-grain white rice
2 tablespoons butter or oil
1 onion, chopped fine
2 cloves garlic, minced
4 cups stock (chicken or beef)

Sauté the rice in the butter or oil until golden brown. Add the onion and sauté until soft, about 5 minutes. Take care not to let the rice burn.

Puree the chiles, garlic, and a little stock until smooth. Add this to the rice and continue cooking over a low heat for 5 minutes.

Stir in the remaining stock and transfer this mixture to a baking dish. Cover and bake at 350°F for 45 minutes. Fluff with a fork before serving.

Serves: 6
Serving Suggestions: This rice can accompany poultry, fish, and red meat dishes. Simply vary the type of stock used.
Variations: Substitute red chiles for the green and you have . . . red rice. Uncover the dish for the final 15 minutes of baking for a crisper rice.
HEAT SCALE: 4

Squash with Corn and Green Chile

(CALIFORNIA)

The staples of pre-Columbian America are combined in this vegetable casserole.

4–5 green chiles, skinned, seeds removed, chopped
1 cup whole kernel corn
2 tablespoons oil
2 onions, chopped
1 clove garlic, minced
4 summer or zucchini squash, diced into cubes
Salt and pepper to taste

Fry the corn in the oil for 5 minutes, stirring constantly so it does not burn. Add the onions, garlic, and chile and cook until the onions are soft. Add the remaining ingredients and cook over a low heat until the squash is tender.

Serves: 6
Serving Suggestions: Baked or broiled meats are enhanced by this side dish.
Variation: To make a casserole, put the cooked squash mixture in a dish, add 1 cup of milk mixed with 2 tablespoons flour, and top with grated cheese. Bake 20 minutes at 325°F.
HEAT SCALE: 4

Spanish Spinach

(NEW MEXICO)

Two favorites, chiles and pinto beans, are combined with spinach in this traditional New Mexican dish.

1 tablespoon dried chile seeds or dried red chile, crushed
3 tablespoons onion, chopped
2 cloves garlic, minced
2 tablespoons bacon drippings
1 pound spinach, cooked and drained
1/2 cup pinto beans, cooked
1 teaspoon vinegar
Salt

Sauté the onions and garlic in the bacon drippings until soft. Add the remaining ingredients and fry for 10 to 15 minutes.

Serves: 4
HEAT SCALE: 3

5
Mexico

Mexico probably has the most diverse hot food cuisine of any country, yet it contains but one fiery ingredient: chiles. Literally hundreds of varieties of *Capsicum annuum* grow in Mexico, and they are served in uncountable dozens of ways: fresh, dried, pickled, in salsas, stews, seafood, meats, moles, soups, and vegetables. In fact, meals served in Mexico are as diverse as those of the United States or China, yet few people realize it because when they hear the term "Mexican food," they think only of tacos. Of course, as we've mentioned before, tacos and enchiladas *are* Mexican, originating from the arid northern states of Chihuahua and Sonora. In the central and southern parts of the country one finds seafood, vegetables, and poultry prepared with imagination and great care.

In the recipes that follow we have attempted to specify the particular variety of chile used for each dish, but there is great latitude here. Often particular kinds of dried chiles are unavailable in certain regions, so reasonable substitutions must be made. Use fresh or canned green chile when varieties like serrano are required, and dried red pods or powder from New Mexico when you cannot locate pasilla, ancho, mulato, or other dried Mexican chiles.

Frijoles Para Sopear
Bean Dip

This party dip is best when served warm.

4 green chiles, skinned, seeds removed, chopped
¹/₂ cup green chile sauce (see p. 30)
3 cups refried beans (cooked pinto beans that have been mashed
   and fried in oil)
1 small onion, chopped
1 cup cheddar or Monterey Jack cheese, grated
Salt to taste

In a saucepan, heat the beans until very hot. Add all the other ingredients and stir until the cheese melts. Add water, if necessary, to thin to the desired consistency for dipping.

Yield: 3 to 3¹/₂ cups
Serving Suggestions: Serve in a chafing dish as an appetizer or hors d'oeuvre with corn or tortilla chips.
HEAT SCALE: 4

Guacamole

Avocado Salad

There are a number of variations of this tasty dish in both Mexico and the Sunbelt, and most contain chiles in some form. Recommended are fresh green chiles, but canned or fresh jalapeños or serranos may be used.

3 green chiles, skinned, seeds removed, chopped fine
1 tomato, chopped fine
3 ripe avocados, mashed
1 medium onion, chopped fine
¹/₄ teaspoon garlic powder (or more)
Pinch each cumin and dried oregano (optional)
Juice of 1 lemon
Salt to taste

Combine all ingredients and mix well.

Yield: 2 to 3 cups
Serving Suggestions: Serve over chopped lettuce as a salad,
or as a dip with tostadas or corn chips. Use as a topping for
chimichangas, enchiladas, burritos, and tostadas.
HEAT SCALE: 3

Shrimp-Stuffed Avocados

From the vast coastal regions of Mexico comes this spicy shrimp salad
that is great as a luncheon entrée or in smaller portions as an
appetizer.

3–4 green chiles, skinned, seeds removed, chopped
1 1/2 tablespoons red chile sauce (see p. 31)
1/2 cup mayonnaise
3 tablespoons onion, chopped fine
1 clove garlic, minced
1 pound cooked shrimp, shelled
2 avocados, halved

Mix together the chiles, chile sauce, mayonnaise, onions, and
garlic. Add the shrimp, toss until well coated, and marinate
overnight. When ready to serve, divide shrimp mixture evenly
among avocado halves.

Serves: 4 as an entrée
Serving Suggestions: Garnish with parsley or fresh cilantro.
Note: This recipe requires advance preparation.
HEAT SCALE: 4

Chicken Corn Soup

Three staples of the cuisine, chile, chicken, and corn, are combined in this simple to prepare soup.

4 green chiles, skinned, seeds removed, chopped
1 small onion, chopped
2 tablespoons butter or margarine
1/2 cup cooked diced potatoes
2 cups cooked diced chicken
1 cup cooked whole kernel corn
4 cups chicken broth
Salt to taste

Sauté the onion in the butter until soft. Add all the remaining ingredients and simmer covered for 30 minutes.

Serves: 4
Serving Suggestions: Excellent as a luncheon entrée served with sliced avocados and flour tortillas or as an accompaniment to a light dinner of cheese enchiladas and rice.
Variations: Stir in 1/2 cup heavy cream just before serving.
HEAT SCALE: 4

Mole Sauce

Pronounced "*mo*-lay," this subtle blend of chocolate with chile is often called the "National Dish of Mexico" when combined with turkey and can be used in a number of ways.

4 dried red chile pods, seeds removed
4 dried pasilla or mulato chiles, seeds removed
1 medium onion, chopped
2 cloves garlic, chopped
2 medium tomatoes (red or green), peeled and chopped
2 tablespoons sesame seeds
¹/₂ cup almonds
¹/₂ corn tortilla, torn into pieces
¹/₄ cup raisins
¹/₄ teaspoon each cloves, cinnamon, and coriander
3 tablespoons lard or shortening
1 cup chicken broth
1 ounce bitter chocolate (or more to taste)
Salt to taste

Combine the chiles, onion, garlic, tomatoes, 1 tablespoon of the sesame seeds, almonds, tortilla, raisins, cloves, cinnamon, and coriander. Puree this mixture in a blender, small amounts at a time, until smooth.

Melt the lard in a skillet and sauté the puree for 10 minutes, stirring frequently. Add the chicken broth, chocolate, and salt and cook over a very low heat for 45 minutes. The sauce should be very thick. The remaining sesame seeds are used as a garnish.

Yield: 4 cups
Serving Suggestions: This sauce is excellent with poultry—serve it over turkey breast and garnish with the remaining sesame seeds. Also excellent as an enchilada sauce over shredded chicken or turkey enchiladas.
HEAT SCALE: 4

Salsa Borracha

Freely translated, "salsa borracha" means drunken sauce; it gets its name from the tequila.

6–8 fresh green chiles, skinned, seeds removed
2 tablespoons oil
1 medium onion, chopped
1 clove garlic, chopped
1 cup orange juice
¼ cup tequila
Salt to taste

Sauté the chiles in oil for 10 minutes over a low heat and remove. Sauté the onion and garlic in the oil until soft.

Blend the chiles and orange juice in a blender until smooth. Add to the onion and cook for an additional 10 minutes. Add the tequila just before serving, being careful not to let it boil.

Yield: 2½ cups
Serving Suggestions: This is a very versatile sauce that is used as a barbecue sauce or a marinade for pork, lamb, chicken, or beef.
Variations: Use ¾ cup orange and ¼ cup lemon or lime juice. Substitute mescal or rum in place of the tequila. For a sweeter sauce, add 1 to 2 teaspoons honey. Substitute pasilla chiles for the green chiles.
HEAT SCALE: 7

Mole de Olla

Kettle Stew

Mole means "mixture" in Spanish, so the word crops up in recipes that have nothing to do with the traditional chocolate mole sauce. Here is a mole or stew that is as tasty as it is unusual.

4 or 5 green chiles, skinned, seeds removed, chopped
1 1/2 pounds stew beef, cubed
2 tablespoons vegetable oil
2 medium onions, chopped
1 clove garlic, chopped
1/2 teaspoon cinnamon
1/4 teaspoon ground cloves
3 cups water
1 cup raw corn
1 cup green beans
4 crookneck or zucchini squash, cut into 1-inch cubes
Salt to taste

Brown the meat in the oil. Puree the chiles, onions, garlic, cinnamon, and cloves in 1 cup of water. Combine the remaining water, meat, corn, beans, and chile mixture and simmer for 1 hour.

Add the squash and cook the stew for an additional half-hour. Add more water if necessary, but the stew should be fairly thick.

Serves: 4
Serving Suggestions: Serve with corn bread or flour tortillas and a green salad—kettle stew can be a meal in itself.
HEAT SCALE: 4

Enchiladas

Enchiladas are one of the most popular of all Mexican dishes and also one of the most bastardized. Those served at fast-food operations are mass merchandised and are made as bland as possible so as not to offend the meat-and-potatoes palate. The enchiladas here are from traditional recipes served in Chihuahua. They may be served flat, with the stuffing between each layer of tortillas, or the tortillas may be rolled with the stuffing inside.

3 cups red or green chile sauce (pp. 30-31)
12 corn tortillas
1/2 cup oil
1 1/2 cups cooked meat (ground beef, chicken, or pork)
2 cups grated cheese (cheddar, Monterey Jack, or longhorn)
1 large onion, chopped fine
Shredded lettuce and chopped tomato for garnish

Fry each tortilla in hot oil for a few seconds until it is soft. Do not overcook them or they will get crisp. Drain on paper towels.

Add the filling to the tortillas: (1) For rolled enchiladas, place some of the meat, cheese, and onion on a tortilla and roll it up. Place three rolled enchiladas on a plate, cover with chile sauce, and sprinkle them with more cheese and onion. (2) For stacked enchiladas, place the meat, cheese, and onion and a little sauce between layers of tortillas on a plate, cover with chile sauce, and sprinkle with cheese and onion.

Heat the enchilada plates in an oven or under a broiler until the cheese just begins to brown.

Serves: 4
Serving Suggestions: There are numerous ways to serve enchiladas. Garnish them with shredded lettuce and chopped tomatoes before serving. Smother them with guacamole (p. 51) and garnish with sour cream. Often enchiladas are served with a fried egg on top. They go well with rice and beans.

Variations: Enchilada casseroles are large numbers of rolled enchiladas stacked in a casserole dish, baked in a chile sauce, and topped with cheese. Bake for 1 hour at 350°F. For a dessert enchilada, slice half a banana lengthwise and fry in butter. Roll each section of banana in a tortilla, cover with mole sauce (p. 54) and bake at 350°F for 15 minutes.

HEAT SCALE: 4

Carne Asada

Carne asada refers to meat that is roasted, broiled, or barbecued. Our recipe calls for the meat to be marinated overnight before being broiled.

1 cup green chile sauce (see p. 30)
1 teaspoon dry mustard
1 teaspoon Worcestershire sauce
1 small onion, chopped
4 tablespoons red wine
4 tablespoons oil
2 tablespoons sugar
2 tablespoons lime juice
1/2 teaspoon salt
1 1/2 pounds flank steak, 1 1/2 inches thick

Combine all ingredients except the steak and simmer for 15 minutes, then cool. Add the steak and marinate in the sauce overnight.

Remove the steak and save the marinade. Broil or grill the steak and heat the marinade separately.

Serves: 4 to 6
Serving Suggestions: Carve the steak slantwise across the grain in thin strips (as you would London broil) and serve with the sauce on the side, accompanied by green rice (see p. 47).
Note: This recipe requires advance preparation.
HEAT SCALE: 5

Carnero Adobo

Beef or pork can be substituted for the lamb in this dish. Adobo refers to the thick sauce or paste of chiles, vinegar, and spices.

6 dried red chiles or 4 pasilla chiles
2 pounds boneless lamb cut in 1-inch cubes
2 cloves garlic, minced
2 medium onions, chopped
3–4 sprigs fresh cilantro
Water
Salt to taste
1/4 teaspoon ground cumin
1/2 teaspoon dried oregano, crushed
2 tablespoons red wine vinegar
3 tablespoons lard or shortening

Place the lamb in a heavy saucepan or casserole with half the garlic and onion, the cilantro, salt, and water to barely cover. Bring to a boil, reduce the heat, cover, and simmer until the meat is tender, about 1½ hours. Remove the lamb, strain the stock, and reserve.

Place the chiles, remaining onion and garlic, cumin, oregano, vinegar, and salt in a blender and puree until the mixture is a fairly smooth paste.

Sauté the chile mixture in the lard, stirring constantly for 5 minutes. Thin the mixture with 1½ cups of the reserved lamb stock until it is the consistency of a medium white sauce. Add the lamb to the sauce and simmer over low heat for 20 minutes.

Serves: 6 to 8
HEAT SCALE: 5

Javelina Roast

The pork in this pre-Columbian recipe is that of the javelina, or peccary, which was a staple in Mexico before the advent of the domesticated pig. We have substituted a pork roast for the wild pig.

1/2 cup red chile sauce (see p. 31)
4-pound pork roast
2 cloves garlic, chopped fine
1/2 teaspoon dried oregano, crushed
1/2 teaspoon dried sage, crushed
3 tablespoons onion, chopped fine
4 tablespoons flour
1/2 cup tomato sauce
1/2 cup raisins (optional)
2 teaspoons salt
Water

Mix the garlic, oregano, sage, and salt together and rub the mixture into the roast. Place the meat, fat side up, in a pan and roast at 350°F for 2 hours. Remove the roast and keep warm.

Pour the drippings into a skillet, add the onion, and sauté until the onion is transparent. Thicken the drippings with the flour and add the chile sauce, tomato sauce, and raisins. Add enough water to achieve the desired consistency and simmer the mixture for 10 minutes.

Return the roast to the pan, baste with the sauce, and roast an additional 30 minutes, basting two or three times with the sauce.

Serves: 6 to 8
Serving Suggestions: Served sliced and covered with the remaining sauce, accompanied by roast potatoes or green rice.
HEAT SCALE: 4

Pollo Pasilla

The sweetness of the honey is cut by the heat of the chiles and the sourness of the lemon or lime juice. Translation: chicken with pasilla chiles.

6–8 pasilla or red chiles, seeds removed
2 cups water
6 chicken thighs or 4 chicken breasts
1/2 cup butter
1 onion, chopped fine
1/2 cup honey
Juice of 2 lemons or limes

Soak the chiles in the 2 cups of hot water.

Brown the chicken in half the butter, turning frequently, and remove. Sauté the onion in the remaining butter until browned.

Puree the chiles in water, honey, and lemon or lime juice until smooth. Add the mixture to the browned onions and cook over low heat for 10 minutes.

Place the chicken in a broiling pan, baste with the sauce, and bake at 350°F for 30 minutes or until the chicken is done, basting frequently with the sauce.

Serves: 4
Serving Suggestions: Garnish this "red" chicken with orange slices and serve with rice.
HEAT SCALE: 5

Chicken with Lime Sauce

Don't let the long list of ingredients scare you off. This dish requires some work, but it is well worth the extra effort.

4 green chiles, skinned, seeds removed, chopped
4 boneless chicken breasts
3 tablespoons flour, plus flour to dredge the chicken
8 tablespoons butter
1/2 cup tequila
Grated rinds of 2 large limes
2 cloves garlic, minced
1 cup chicken stock or broth
1 cup sour cream
1 cup heavy cream
Juice of 2 limes
2 teaspoons sugar
1/3 cup Parmesan cheese, grated
Salt and white pepper to taste

Dredge the chicken in flour and quickly brown in 5 tablespoons of the butter. Pour 1/4 cup of the tequila over the chicken and light. When the flame dies down, remove the chicken and set aside.

Add the remaining butter to the pan the chicken was browned in and heat. Slowly add the chiles, lime rind, and garlic and cook for 4 minutes. Add the flour, 1/4 cup tequila, and the chicken stock. Slowly bring the mixture to a boil, stirring constantly. Immediately reduce the heat and simmer for 5 minutes. Fold the sour cream and heavy cream into the sauce and add the lime juice and sugar.

Place the chicken back into the pan, cover with the sauce, and simmer until tender, about 30 minutes.

When done, place the chicken in a serving dish, cover with the sauce, and top with the Parmesan cheese. Place under the broiler only long enough to brown the cheese.

Serves: 4

Serving Suggestions: Since this dish is so rich, simple accompaniments like a salad and plain vegetable are best.

HEAT SCALE: 3

Guatemalan Red Snapper

At first the combination of hot chiles with fish seems unusual, but in reality similar dishes appear in cuisines worldwide. Virtually any fresh or canned chiles will work in this well-known Mexican dish—jalapeños or serranos are recommended.

5 green chiles, skinned, seeds removed, chopped
6 red snapper fillets
4 tablespoons lime or lemon juice
Flour seasoned with thyme
1 medium onion, chopped
2 cloves garlic, minced
2–3 tablespoons olive oil
3 tomatoes, peeled and chopped
1/4 cup tomato puree
1/4 teaspoon cinnamon
1/4 teaspoon ground cloves
1 cup water
Stuffed green olives, sliced

Rub the fish with the lime or lemon juice and lightly coat with seasoned flour. Sauté the fish on both sides in olive oil until golden brown. Remove, set aside, and keep warm.

Sauté the onion and garlic in the oil until soft. Add the remaining ingredients except the fish and simmer for 20 minutes.

Place the fish in a large pan, cover with the sauce, and heat. Garnish with the sliced green olives and serve.

Serves: 6
Serving Suggestions: This fish is excellent with rice and green beans.

HEAT SCALE: 4

Fish in Chile Almond Sauce

With over 5000 miles of coastland and lakes, it is easy to see why fish dishes are popular in Mexico.

4 serrano or jalapeño chiles, chopped
2 cups water or court bouillon
6 snapper or flounder fillets
1 clove garlic
1 slice white bread, crusts removed
1/2 cup blanched almonds
1/2 cup fresh cilantro or parsley, chopped
Salt and pepper to taste

Bring the water or bouillon to a boil and add the fillets. Reduce the heat, cover, and simmer until the fish flakes easily but does not fall apart, about 8 to 10 minutes. Remove the fish and retain the bouillon.

Combine the chiles, garlic, bread, almonds, cilantro, and bouillon in a blender and puree until smooth. Transfer the mixture to a pan and simmer until the sauce thickens. Pour the sauce over the fish and serve.

Serves: 6
Serving Suggestions: Arrange the fish on a bed of rice, pour the sauce over the top, and garnish with additional almond slices. Serve with baked yams for color.
HEAT SCALE: 3

Huevos con Chorizo

Eggs with Hot Sausage

Chorizos are very hot, spicy sausages that are made from beef or pork or a combination of both. They are seasoned with garlic, cayenne, and chile powder.

3 green chiles, skinned, seeds removed, chopped
1 onion, chopped fine
1 tablespoon butter
1 clove garlic, minced
2 chorizo sausages, skinned and chopped
3 tomatoes, peeled and chopped
Pinch of sugar
Salt and pepper to taste
6 eggs, slightly beaten

Sauté the onion in the butter until soft. Add the garlic and the sausage and continue cooking for five minutes. Add the tomatoes, sugar, salt, and pepper and cook for an additional 5 minutes. Slowly stir in the eggs and cook until the eggs are set and done.

Serves: 4
Serving Suggestions: Eggs with chorizos are excellent as a brunch entrée. Serve with flour tortillas, fresh fruit compote, and Mexican hot chocolate.

HEAT SCALE: 4

Huevos Rancheros

There are many variations of this popular dish—ranch-style eggs. We have included this easy favorite of ours.

2 cups green or red chile sauce (pp. 30-31)
3 fresh green or red chiles, skinned, seeds removed, chopped
4 eggs
4 corn tortillas
Oil for frying
¹/₂ cup cheddar cheese, grated

Heat the chile sauce in a shallow frying pan. Carefully slip the eggs into the hot sauce and poach to the desired firmness.

Fry each tortilla in hot oil only for a few seconds until soft, then drain.

Place the eggs and sauce on the tortillas. Mound additional sauce around the edges and sprinkle the chopped chiles over the sauce. Top with the grated cheese and serve immediately.

Serves: 2 to 4

Serving Suggestions: Serve with potatoes and chile (p. 46), flour tortillas, and refried beans, and garnish the plate with avocado slices.

HEAT SCALE: 6

Arroz con Queso

Plain rice is transformed into a savory side dish with the addition of chile and cheese in this simple recipe.

4 green chiles, skinned, seeds removed, chopped
1 cup sour cream
2 cups cooked rice
1 cup cheddar cheese, grated

Combine the green chiles and sour cream in a bowl. Add the cooked rice and mix well. Pour this mixture into a greased pan and top with the grated cheese. Bake at 350°F for 15 to 20 minutes or until thoroughly heated and the cheese has melted.

Serves: 4
Serving Suggestions: Goes well with plain fish, poultry, or meat.
HEAT SCALE: 3

Spicy Green Beans

These beans go well with cheese dishes or simple meats but can add color and heat to any meal.

3–4 green chiles, skinned, seeds removed, chopped
1 medium onion, chopped
1 clove garlic, chopped
1 tablespoon oil or lard
1 pound green beans
2 tomatoes, peeled and chopped
1 cup water
Salt to taste

Sauté the onion and garlic in the oil until soft. Add the chiles and fry for 2 or 3 more minutes. Add the remaining ingredients, bring to a boil, reduce the heat, and simmer until the beans are done.

Serves: 4
HEAT SCALE: 4

Elote con Crema

Translated from Spanish, elote con crema means "corn with cream."

4–5 green chiles, skinned, seeds removed, chopped
1 small onion, chopped
1 clove garlic, chopped fine
2 tablespoon butter
4 cups whole kernel corn
Salt and pepper to taste
1/4 cup Monterey Jack or cheddar cheese, cut into small cubes
Sour cream for garnishing

Sauté the onion and garlic in the butter until soft. Add the chiles and cook for an additional 8 to 10 minutes. Stir in the corn, salt, and pepper and transfer the mixture to a baking dish.

Add the cheese cubes to the casserole and bake at 300°F for 40 minutes.

Top with the sour cream before serving.

Serves: 4 to 6
Serving Suggestions: This side dish can be served either as a vegetable dish to accompany meats or as a starch to replace potatoes or rice.
Variations: Add sliced zucchini and cooked peeled potatoes.
HEAT SCALE: 4

Baked Carrots

Jalapeños more often appear in uncooked dishes, but this unusual vegetable recipe shows their versatility.

2 jalapeño chiles, sliced in rings
1 pound carrots, cut in thin "coins"
1/2 cup water
Salt to taste
2 tablespoons butter or margarine
1/4 teaspoon cinnamon

Place the carrots and chiles in a baking dish. Add the water, salt to taste, and dot with the butter and cinnamon.

Bake, covered, in a 350°F oven until done, about 1 hour.

Serves: 4
HEAT SCALE: 4

6
The Caribbean

Because of the patterns of European colonization, the West Indies contain such a wide range of food styles that the food of the area can hardly be termed a cuisine. When Columbus landed in these islands, he did, indeed, "discover" chiles so far as the Old World was concerned. He took back seeds that eventually spread the cultivation of *Capsicum annuum* around the world. But on the isles of the Caribbean, the Indians were already cooking with them. The first settlers of these islands, the Arawaks and the Caribs, apparently brought chiles with them from South America and began cultivation. Then the Spanish, English, Dutch, and French colonists brought their foods to the islands, and the African slaves added theirs. Quite a combination!

The most common hot ingredients used on the islands include green chiles and curries, which utilize the smaller hot chiles like serranos and jalapeños. Chiles are most often combined with poultry, seafoods, goat, vegetables, and rice. Curiously, ginger, which is grown extensively in Jamaica, is not utilized in many island recipes.

Yam Crisps

(JAMAICA)

Traditionally served as an hors d'oeuvre, yam crisps are an unusual delicacy.

2 teaspoons ground red chile
4 yams
1/2 cup brown sugar
1/2 cup cracker crumbs
1/2 cup butter

Bake the yams in their skins in a 350°F oven for 1 hour. Cool, peel, and cut into thin strips about 1 by 2 inches.

Combine the brown sugar, chile, and cracker crumbs. Dip the yams strips in the mixture and toss until well coated. Fry the strips in hot butter, turning often until browned on all sides.

Serves: 8
HEAT SCALE: 2

Fish in Escabeche

(CUBA)

Escabeche is a Spanish word meaning "pickled." It also describes a dish popular in many Spanish-speaking countries where a fish is first cooked, then marinated in a spicy vinegar sauce.

4 dried santaka chiles, whole
2 pounds firm white fish, cubed
1/4 cup olive oil
2 medium onions, sliced
2 cloves garlic, chopped
2/3 cup red wine vinegar
1/4 teaspoon thyme
1/4 teaspoon majoram
3 whole peppercorns

Fry the fish cubes in the oil until lightly browned. Remove and drain.

Sauté the onion and garlic in the remaining oil until soft. Place the fish in a glass or ceramic pan and top with the onions, garlic, and oil.

Heat the wine vinegar with the remaining ingredients and simmer for 15 minutes.

Pour the vinegar marinade over the fish and marinate in the refrigerator for 24 hours.

Serves: 8
Serving Suggestions: Garnish with sliced green olives and serve as an appetizer.
Note: This recipe requires advance preparation.
HEAT SCALE: 4

Chile Conch Salad

(BAHAMAS)

In this recipe we are using an acid to "cook" the raw fish. It is important to use either a glass or ceramic bowl—a metal container will produce a metallic taste.

4 serrano or jalapeño chiles, chopped fine
1/2 teaspoon freshly ground black pepper
2 cups conch meat, pounded until tender and then chopped, or
    abalone (treated in the same way)
1/4 cup pimiento, chopped
2 tomatoes, peeled and chopped fine
2 cloves garlic, minced
1 medium onion, chopped fine
1/2 cup celery, chopped fine
1/2 cup lime juice
3 tablespoons oil
1/4 teaspoon dried oregano, crushed
Salt to taste

Combine all the ingredients and toss gently until well coated. Marinate the mixture in the refrigerator for at least 6 hours or until the conch becomes opaque.

Serves: 4
Note: This recipe requires advance preparation.
HEAT SCALE: 6

Spicy Chicken Soup

(CURAÇAO)

Here is a soup from the Netherlands Antilles that verges on being a full-fledged stew. It is definitely a meal in itself.

4–5 green chiles, skinned, seeds removed, chopped
Whole chicken, 2–3 pounds
2 quarts chicken stock
2 potatoes, peeled and diced
1 cup peas
2 yams, peeled and diced
3 tomatoes, peeled and chopped
1/4 pound hubbard squash, diced
1 cup whole kernel corn
1/2 cup onion, diced
Salt and pepper to taste

Combine the chicken and stock and bring to a boil. Reduce the heat, cover, and simmer for one hour or until the chicken is done. Skim off any foam that surfaces. Remove the chicken, pull the meat from the bones, and chop. Reserve the stock.

Allow the stock to cool in the refrigerator and remove the fat that rises. Return the chopped chicken, add the remaining ingredients, and bring to a boil. Reduce the heat and simmer until the vegetables are tender, about 30 minutes.

Serves: 6 to 8
HEAT SCALE: 4

Jamaican Red Bean Soup

The combination of beans and soup is very common in the islands, and the soups are usually quite pungent.

6 serrano or jalapeño chiles, chopped
2 cups dried kidney beans
1 medium onion, chopped
2 stalks celery, chopped
1/4 pound salt pork
1 1/2 quarts water
Salt and pepper to taste

Combine all the ingredients in a large pot or crock pot. Bring to a boil, reduce the heat, and simmer for 3 hours or until the beans are done. Add more water if necessary.

Puree until smooth and strain. The soup should be thick. Reheat the soup before serving.

Serves: 6
HEAT SCALE: 6

Chile Seafood Sauce

(GUADALOUPE)

There are an infinite number of variations of island sauces that accompany seafood or poultry. Lime juice and chiles are a common combination.

2 serrano or jalapeño chiles, chopped fine
1 medium onion, chopped fine
Juice of 2 limes
2 tablespoons butter
1 clove garlic, mashed or minced
Salt to taste

Marinate the onion in the lime juice for 1 hour, then drain and save the marinade.

Sauté the onion in the butter until soft. Add the garlic, chiles, lime marinade, and salt. Cook over a low heat for 15 minutes and cool before serving.

Yield: 1 cup
Serving Suggestions: Excellent with broiled fish or chicken.
HEAT SCALE: 3

Pepper Sauce
(HAITI)

This fiery sauce is traditionally served as an accompaniment to fish or poultry.

$^1/_2$ *cup chiles (jalapeños or serranos), chopped fine*
$^1/_2$ *cup papaya, chopped fine*
1 *cup onions, chopped fine*
3 *cloves garlic, chopped fine*
$^1/_2$ *teaspoon turmeric*
$^1/_4$ *cup malt vinegar*
1 *teaspoon salt*

Combine all the ingredients in a saucepan and bring to a boil, stirring constantly. Reduce the heat and cook for an additional 5 minutes. Put the mixture in a blender and puree until smooth.

Allow to cool to room temperature before serving.

Yield: 1 to $^1/_2$ cups
HEAT SCALE: 7

Chile Pot

(TRINIDAD AND TOBAGO)

This is a modern adaptation of the Trinidadian recipe that traditionally requires the addition of cassareep, which is an extract of cassava root.

4–5 fresh red or green chiles, skinned, seeds removed, chopped
3-pound chicken, cut into serving pieces
3 cups water
Salt to taste
1 pound pork or beef, cut in 1-inch cubes
1 large onion, coarsely chopped
3 tablespoons brown sugar
1 stick cinnamon
6 whole cloves
1/4 teaspoon thyme
1 tablespoon vinegar

Cover the chicken with salted water and bring to a boil. Boil for 10 minutes, skimming off any foam as it forms. Reduce the heat and simmer for 1 hour. Remove from the heat and allow the stock to cool. Skim off any fat that rises to the top. Remove the chicken from the bone and chop.

Add all the ingredients except the vinegar to the stock and simmer for an additional 45 minutes to 1 hour or until the meat is tender. Add the vinegar just before serving.

Serves: 6
Serving Suggestions: Serve with baked yams or sweet potatoes.
HEAT SCALE: 4

Ropa Vieja Cubana

Cuban "Old Clothes"

Despite the odd name—an idiom for leftovers—this is an extremely popular dish both in Cuba and among Cubans living in the United States. In some versions it is served with lots of chiles like serranos or jalapeños, in others it is bland. Adjust the pungency to your own taste.

3 teaspoons serrano chiles, chopped fine
2 pounds flank steak
1 large onion, coarsely chopped
1 bay leaf
2 cups water
1 teaspoon salt
2 garlic cloves, chopped fine
2 bell peppers, chopped fine
2 tablespoons olive oil
4 large tomatoes, peeled and chopped
1/4 teaspoon cinnamon
1/2 teaspoon ground cloves
2 carrots, diced

Simmer the steak, half the onion, salt, and the bay leaf in the water for an hour and a half or until the meat is tender. Remove the steak, strain the liquid, and reserve the stock. Cut the steak into strips 1/4 inch wide by 2 to 3 inches long.

Sauté the remaining onion, chiles, garlic, and bell pepper in the olive oil until soft. Stir in the tomatoes, cinnamon, cloves, and the carrots. Cook until the vegetables begin to break down and the mixture is thick.

Add the meat to this sauce along with a cup of the reserved stock and cook until the meat is thoroughly heated.

Serves: 6
Serving Suggestions: Serve with rice and garnish with pimiento strips.
HEAT SCALE: 3

Picadillo
Cuban Hash

There are variations of this dish in virtually every Spanish-speaking country in the Western Hemisphere, though many recipes are not as hot as this one.

5–6 fresh green chiles, skinned, seeds removed, chopped
2 pounds lean beef or pork, cut in 1-inch cubes
2 tablespoons oil
2 onions, chopped fine
2 cloves garlic, chopped fine
3 bell peppers, chopped fine
Salt and papper to taste
6 tomatoes, peeled and chopped
1/4 teaspoon ground cloves
1/2 cup raisins
6 stuffed green olives, sliced
1/4 teaspoon ground cinnamon
2 tablespoons red wine vinegar
1/4 cup blanched almonds, chopped

Brown the meat in the oil. Add the onion, chiles, garlic, bell pepper, salt, and pepper, and sauté for 5 minutes or until the vegetables are soft. Add the remaining ingredients, except for the almonds, and simmer over low heat for 25 to 30 minutes or until the meat is tender.

Sprinkle the almonds over the hash before serving.

Serves: 4 to 6
Variations: Add sliced bananas and chopped pineapple and cook for 15 minutes, then garnish with almonds.
Serving Suggestions: Picadillo is a meal itself, but is also excellent with baked yams or sweet potatoes and rice.
HEAT SCALE: 4

Calabaza Stew

(PUERTO RICO)

Served with fresh, crusty rolls or corn bread, this hearty stew combines several staples of the island: pork, squash, yams, and plantains.

3–4 fresh green chiles, skinned, seeds removed, chopped
2 pounds pork, cut in cubes
1 quart water
1 sweet potato, peeled and sliced
1 yam, peeled and sliced
1 butternut or hubbard squash, cubed
2 medium onions, chopped
2 cloves garlic, chopped
1 bell pepper, chopped
1/4 cup oil
2 medium tomatoes, peeled and chopped
2 zucchinis, cubed
2 plantains or bananas, sliced
Juice of 2 limes

Bring the pork and water to a boil, reduce the heat, and simmer covered for 45 minutes. Add the sweet potato, yam, and butternut squash and simmer for an additional 15 minutes.

Sauté the onion, garlic, bell pepper, and chile in the oil until soft. Add the onion mixture to the meat. Add the tomatoes, zucchini, and plantains and continue to simmer until the squash is tender—about 15 to 20 minutes. Stir in the lime juice and serve.

Serves: 4 to 6
HEAT SCALE: 3

Chile Veal

(ST. LUCIA)

The African influence on Caribbean cooking is illustrated here with the combination of chiles and peanuts.

2 fresh red chiles, skinned, seeds removed, chopped fine
4 veal chops or lamb chops
4 tablespoons peanut butter
1 tablespoon oil
4 green onions, sliced
2 cloves garlic, chopped
1 cup white wine

Cover the veal with the peanut butter and let stand for an hour.

Fry the chops in the oil and remove from the pan. Sauté the onions and garlic in the pan juices until the onions are soft. Add the wine, chile, and chops and cook slowly for 20 minutes, turning occasionally.

Serves: 4
HEAT SCALE: 2

Spiced Meatloaf

(ST. CROIX)

Ah, an exotic variation of that old American favorite! Instead of serving with mashed potatoes, try baked plantains or yams.

1/2 cup red chili sauce (see p. 31)
2 tablespoons mustard powder
2 pounds ground beef or pork
1 medium onion, chopped
1 egg, beaten
1 cup bread crumbs
Salt and pepper to taste
1 cup water
1/2 cup tomato sauce
2 tablespoons vinegar
2 tablespoons brown sugar
2 tablespoons pineapple juice
Pineapple rings

Combine the beef, onion, egg, bread crumbs, salt, pepper, and chile sauce. Form into a loaf and place in a baking pan.

Make a sauce of the mustard, water, tomato sauce, vinegar, sugar, and pineapple juice. Spread this sauce over the top of the loaf and top with the pineapple rings.

Bake at 350°F for 1½ hours, basting frequently with the juices.

Serves: 6 to 8
HEAT SCALE: 2

Curried Goat

(JAMAICA)

This is a traditional celebration dish in Jamaica. Some variations add coconut milk to the recipe or substitute lamb for the goat.

4 serrano chiles, chopped fine
2 tablespoons curry powder (p. 19)
3 pounds lean cabrito (young goat) cut into 1-inch cubes
3 tablespoons butter
2 tablespoons oil
2 onions, chopped fine
1/2 teaspoon allspice
Salt and pepper to taste
1 cup chicken stock
1 bay leaf
2 tablespoons lime juice

Heat 1 tablespoon butter in the oil and brown the goat cubes, turning often. Remove the browned meat and keep warm.

Add the remaining butter and sauté the onion until soft. Add the chiles, allspice, curry powder, salt, and pepper and cook for five minutes over a low heat, stirring constantly.

Then add the meat, stock, and bay leaf and simmer for 1 1/2 hours, or until the meat is tender. Remove the bay leaf, stir in the lime juice, and serve.

Serves: 6 to 8
Serving Suggestions: Serve the meat over rice with the sauce from the pan poured over the top. Garnish with fresh slices of papaya and mango.
HEAT SCALE: 4

Arroz con Pollo

(DOMINICAN REPUBLIC)

This rice and chicken recipe is found everywhere in the Caribbean, although of course it varies a bit from country to country. This particular recipe is interesting because the chicken is marinated first in a hot chile sauce from the adjoining country on the same island.

½ cup Haitian pepper sauce (p. 76)
2-pound chicken, cut into serving pieces
4 tablespoons oil
1 cup rice
2 cups chicken broth
1 bell pepper, chopped
1 cup peas
¼ cup pimientos, chopped

Pour the pepper sauce over the chicken and let stand at room temperature for 2 hours. Remove the chicken and save the marinade.

Heat the oil and fry the chicken pieces until lightly browned. Remove the chicken. Add the rice and sauté until lightly browned. Stir in the remaining ingredients, including the marinade. Add the chicken, cover, and cook over a low heat until the rice is done and the chicken is tender, about 30 minutes.

Serves: 4 to 6
Note: This recipe requires advance preparation.
HEAT SCALE: 5

Cuban Lobster Creole

This hot dish is best served with saffron rice and garnished with parsley.

3 serrano chiles, chopped fine
2 cups chile seafood sauce (p. 75)
2 pounds cooked lobster meat, diced
4 tablespoons oil
1 1/2 cups white wine
1/2 teaspoon dried oregano, crushed
Chopped parsley for garnish

Sauté the lobster and chile in the hot oil for 5 minutes, stirring constantly. Remove the lobster.

Pour off all but 2 teaspoons of the oil and add the wine. Bring to a boil, reduce the heat, and add the seafood sauce and oregano. Simmer the mixture for 3 minutes.

Return the lobster to the pan and cook for 10 minutes basting frequently. Garnish with parsley before serving.

Serves: 4 to 6
HEAT SCALE: 5

Shrimp in Spicy Sauce

(ST. VINCENT)

Lobster may be substituted for shrimp in this fiery seafood dish.

4 teaspoons serrano or jalapeño chiles, seeds removed, chopped
  fine
1/2 cup onions, chopped fine
1/2 cup celery, chopped fine
2 tablespoons oil
4 tomatoes, peeled and chopped
1 bay leaf
1 tablespoon parsley, chopped fine
1 teaspoon sugar
Salt and pepper to taste
2 pounds raw shrimp, peeled and deveined
Grated Parmesan cheese

Sauté the chiles, onions, and celery in oil until the onions are
soft. Add the tomatoes, bay leaf, parsley, sugar, salt, and pepper
and cook until most of the liquid has evaporated and the sauce is
quite thick. Reduce the heat, add the shrimp, cover, and simmer
for about 10 minutes, being careful not to overcook. Garnish
with Parmesan cheese before serving.

Serves: 4 to 6
Serving Suggestions: Serve over rice.
HEAT SCALE: 7

Salt Fish and Ackee

Jamaica's "National Dish"

Ackee is a firm, nutlike substance found inside the fruit of the ackee tree. Oddly enough, other parts of the same fruit are poisonous. It is so prevalent on the island that it is called "free food." Ackee is sometimes found canned in gourmet and specialty shops, but if you can't find it try this substitution: scramble 6 eggs in a nonstick pan without grease until firm. This is stretching it, but the dish still tastes great. Adjust the amount of chile for your heat preference, as this dish is served both pungent and bland.

3 serrano or jalapeño chiles, seeds removed, chopped fine
1 pound salt cod
1 medium onion, chopped fine
2 tablespoons oil
1/4 teaspoon thyme
1/2 pound ackee or substitution

Soak the cod in water to cover for 24 hours, changing the water four or five times to decrease salinity.

Place the cod in a saucepan with just enough fresh water to cover it and boil until the fish begins to flake. Drain and flake the fish, discarding bones, fins and other inedible parts. Set the flaked parts aside.

Sauté the onion and chiles in the oil until the onion is browned, taking care not to allow them to burn. Add the fish, thyme, and ackee and cook over a low heat, stirring often, until thoroughly heated.

Serves: 4
Serving Suggestions: Serve as a breakfast or lunch dish with fresh fruits and rice.
Note: This recipe requires advance preparation.
HEAT SCALE: 3

Pepper Crabs

(DOMINICAN REPUBLIC)

Land crabs are frequently served on the islands by stuffing the empty shells with dishes such as this.

3 teaspoons serrano or jalapeño chiles, chopped fine
1/4 cup bell peppers, chopped fine
1 cup onion, chopped fine
2 cloves garlic, minced
2 tablespoons oil
2 tomatoes, peeled and chopped
1/2 cup dry sherry
3 tablespoons tomato paste
Salt and pepper to taste
1 pound crab meat
1/2 cup lime juice
Chopped parsley for garnish

Sauté the chiles, bell pepper, onion, and garlic in the oil until soft. Add the tomatoes, sherry, tomato paste, salt, and pepper and bring to a boil. Stir the mixture constantly and cook until most of the liquid has evaporated and the sauce begins to hold its shape. Add the crab and stir into the sauce until it is well coated. Reduce the heat, cover, and simmer until the crab is thoroughly heated. Pour the lime juice over the crab and garnish with the parsley.

Serves: 4
HEAT SCALE: 3

7
Latin America

The diverse cuisines of Central and South America resulted from a collision of cultures. Native Indians and black African slaves interacted with the French, Portuguese, German, English, Spanish, Dutch, and even Chinese settlers producing amalgams of cuisines that persist to this day. As might be expected in the land where the fiery fruits originated, chiles are the most important hot ingredient in Latin American meals. However, principally because of the influence of European colonists, horseradish, mustard, and ginger also make their appearance in the dishes that follow.

The combination of seafood and chiles is popular in Central America, along the Caribbean coast of South America, and in Peru and Chile. The cuisine of Central America most resembles that of western and southern Mexico, and the hot cooking of South America depends less on sauces than on dishes where the smaller and hotter chiles are added more for heat than flavor. Hot and spicy vegetable dishes are also a favorite in Latin America—chiles are often added to potatoes, onions, squash, and corn.

Ceviche

(PERU)

There are related raw fish dishes found in countries throughout the world: Peru, Mexico, Ghana, and Spain, to name a few. The lemon or lime juice "cooks" the fish so it doesn't taste raw. Because of the high citric acid content of this dish, always use a ceramic or glass bowl—never a metal one.

4–5 fresh green chiles, skinned, seeds removed, chopped
1½–2 pounds firm white fish (snapper, mackerel, pompano, flounder)
2 cups lime or lemon juice, fresh preferred
1 onion, sliced and separated into rings
½ cup olive oil
1 tablespoon white vinegar
2 cloves garlic, chopped
3 tablespoons fresh parsley, chopped
¼ teaspoon dried oregano
Salt and pepper to taste
4 pimientos, cut into strips

Cover the fish with the lime or lemon juice and refrigerate for 6 hours, turning occasionally until the fish loses its translucency and turns opaque. Drain and reserve the marinade.

Combine all the remaining ingredients except pimiento and add the marinade. Toss the fish in the marinade until well coated and then marinate for 2 more hours. Garnish with the pimiento.

Serves: 6
Serving Suggestions: Serve as a salad over lettuce. In Peru, it is traditionally served as an appetizer for main dishes.
Variations: Substitute scallops, shelled shrimp, or lobster for the white fish.
Note: This recipe requires advance preparation.
HEAT SCALE: 4

Brazilian Marinated Shrimp

This seafood delicacy combines chile, mustard, and horseradish in one recipe.

2 tablespoons red chile, crushed
2 tablespoons prepared mustard
2 teaspoons horseradish sauce (see p. 115)
1/2 cup peanut oil
1/3 cup white vinegar
Juice of 1 lemon or lime
1 pound shrimp, cooked and peeled
1 medium onion, cut into rings and separated
Fresh cilantro or parsley, chopped

Combine the chile, horseradish, mustard, oil, vinegar, and lemon or lime juice and mix well. Add the shrimp and onion rings and toss gently to cover the shrimp. Marinate the shrimp in the refrigerator for 8 hours, turning occasionally.

Drain the shrimp and onions before serving. Garnish with cilantro or parsley.

Serves: 4 to 6
Serving Suggestions: Arrange on a bed of lettuce and serve as a salad or appetizer.
Note: This recipe requires advance preparation.
HEAT SCALE: 4

Chicken-Squash Soup
with Chile Sauce
(BOLIVIA)

Hearty soups are common in South America. Serving the sauce on the side allows the individual to adjust the heat in their soup.

1 cup Chilean hot sauce (see p. 96)
2 pounds chicken, cut in pieces
1 medium onion, coarsely chopped
6 cups water
Salt and pepper to taste
1 pound acorn, butternut, or Hubbard squash, peeled and cut
   into 1-inch cubes
¹/₈ teaspoon turmeric

Bring the chicken, onion, and water to a boil, adding salt and pepper to taste. Skim off any foam that forms. Reduce the heat and simmer until the chicken is tender but not falling off the bones. Remove the chicken and cut the meat off the bones, then chop.

Add the squash and turmeric to the chicken stock and cook covered until the squash is tender, about 20 minutes.

Return the chicken and simmer until thoroughly heated. Heat the hot sauce in a small pan and pour into a serving bowl.

Serves: 6 to 8
Serving Suggestions: Serve the soup and sauce to each individual in separate bowls. The sauce is added to the soup until desired pungency is obtained.

HEAT SCALE: 4

Bahia Peanut Soup

(BRAZIL)

The West African influence is strong in the cooking of Brazil, particularly in the Bahia area. This dish very definitely has an African flavor—note the combination of hot chiles and peanuts.

3 dried santaka chiles, crushed
1 teaspoon powdered ginger
1 teaspoon paprika
1 cup okra, cut in small pieces
1 onion, chopped
4 cups water
Salt to taste
2 pounds dried shrimp, shelled
1/4 cup flour
1 cup roasted cashew nuts
1/2 cup peanut butter

Place the paprika, okra, onion, salt, and water in a pan and bring to a boil. Reduce the heat and cook until the okra is tender.

Puree the dried shrimp until nearly a powder. Mix the shrimp with the flour and cashews until thoroughly blended. Thin the peanut butter with a small amount of water to make a thick paste. Mix the chiles, ginger, shrimp, and peanut butter and heat slowly.

Stir the peanut butter mixture into the okra. Bring to a boil and cook for 15 minutes, stirring constantly.

Serves: 4
HEAT SCALE: 5

Empanaditas

(ARGENTINA)

Variations on these spicy turnover appetizers are found throughout Latin America, Mexico, and the American Southwest. There are an infinite number of combinations of fillings that can be used, so experiment with your own.

FILLING
1 teaspoon dried santaka chiles or 4 chile piquins, crushed, or 1
    teaspoon red chile paste (p. 95)
1/2 cup onion, chopped fine
1 tablespoon oil
1/2 cup water
1/2 pound sirloin steak, coarsely chopped
3 tablespoons raisins
1/4 teaspoon powdered cumin
1/2 teaspoon salt
2 hard-cooked eggs, sliced, for garnish

Combine the onion, oil, and water in a skillet and boil the mixture until the water has evaporated. Add the steak and brown on all sides. Add the raisins, chiles, cumin, and salt. Remove from the heat and set aside. The sliced eggs are not added yet; set them aside as well.

PASTRY
2 1/2 cups flour
1 teaspoon salt
1/2 cup shortening (lard preferred)
1/2 cup water

Combine the flour, salt, and shortening and mix thoroughly with a pastry blender until the mixture has the texture of coarse meal. Add the water and mix until the dough can be gathered in a compact ball. Roll the dough to between 1/8 and 1/4 inch thick. Cut the dough into 5-inch-diameter circles.

TO ASSEMBLE

Place about a tablespoon and a half of filling in the center of each circle of dough and top with an egg slice. Moisten the edges of the dough and fold them together to form a crescent. Press or crimp the edges firmly together to make a seal. Bake on an ungreased sheet pan for 20 minutes at 400°F or until the pastry is cooked and browned.

Yield: 2 dozen
Serving Suggestions: Traditionally served as a hot hors d'oeuvre.
HEAT SCALE: 5

Red Chile Paste

(CHILE AND PERU)

In South American this paste is often used in place of fresh chiles. A word of caution—this is an extremely hot paste, so use sparingly!

1 cup santaka chiles, seeds removed, or red or pasilla chiles for
    a less pungent paste
1 cup boiling water
2 cloves garlic, chopped fine
1 cup chicken stock or broth
1/2 cup oil

Pour the boiling water over the chiles and let stand for 20 minutes or until the chiles are soft.

Drain the chiles and combine with all the other ingredients. Place the mixture in a blender and puree until smooth.

Yield: 1 1/2 cups
Serving Suggestions: Serve as an accompaniment to broiled or roasted meats or with poultry. Place in a small bowl and allow guests to use as much as they dare. Can also be used in sauces and combination entrées when a heat source is required.
HEAT SCALE: 9

Chilean Hot Sauce

Of course, the number of chiles used will determine the heat scale of this sauce, so use as many as you dare.

4 fresh green chiles, skinned, seeds removed, chopped fine, or
   substitute 1 1/2 tablespoons red chile paste (p. 9.)
1 tablespoon red wine vinegar
2 tablespoons oil
1/2 cup water
1 medium onion, chopped fine
2 cloves garlic, chopped fine
1/4 cup fresh cilantro or parsley, chopped
Salt to taste

Beat the vinegar, oil, and water together until combined. Add the remaining ingredients and allow to sit for 3 or 4 hours at room temperature.

Yield: 1 to 1 1/2 cups
Serving Suggestions: Serve to accompany broiled meats, fish, or poultry.
Variation: Use red chiles in place of the green.
Note: This recipe requires advance preparation.
HEAT SCALE: 4

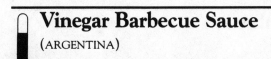

Vinegar Barbecue Sauce

(ARGENTINA)

This very hot sauce appears at barbecue roasts in cattle country—the Pampas. It is not designed for basting but rather to be added to the meat at the table.

3/4 tablespoon santaka chiles, crushed
3/4 cup red wine vinegar
1/4 cup peanut oil
3 cloves garlic, minced
3/4 teaspoon oregano, crushed
Salt and freshly ground pepper

Combine all the ingredients and allow to sit for at least 24 hours to blend all the flavors.

Yield: 1 cup
Serving Suggestions: Try over shish-kabobs or charcoal-broiled beefsteak.
Note: This recipe requires advance preparation.
HEAT SCALE: 8

Matahambre

(ARGENTINA)

The title of this dish translates variously as "jungle hunger" or "starving to death." It is a hearty dish that varies in heat according to the cook. Matahambre is most often served hot, but is also delicious cold.

6 fresh green chiles, skinned, seeds removed, chopped fine
$1/2$ cup beer
$1/2$ cup vinegar
$1/4$ cup oil
1 medium onion, chopped
2 cloves garlic, chopped fine
1 bay leaf
Salt and pepper to taste
2 pounds flank or round steak (one large steak)
2 potatoes, sliced into strips
2 carrots, sliced thinly lengthwise
4 slices bacon

Mix the beer, vinegar, oil, half the onion and garlic, bay leaf, salt, and pepper together. Marinate the steak in the mixture for 3 hours.

Remove the steak and flatten the meat with a rolling pin. Spread the chiles over the meat, then the potatoes, carrots, and bacon. Roll up the steak, taking care to turn the edges in so the stuffing does not fall out. Tie the roll with string to hold it together.

Place the rolled steak in a pan with half the remaining marinade and enough water to come up to the top of the meat. Add the remaining onion and garlic and simmer for $2^{1/2}$ hours.

Serves:　6

Serving Suggestions: Cut the roll into slices and spoon a little of the broth over each slice. Serve with oven-browned potatoes and glazed carrots.

Note: This recipe requires advance preparation.

HEAT SCALE: 3

Churrasco

(BRAZIL)

Churrasco, or barbecue, is common in the southern parts of Brazil where large cattle ranches are located. The barbecue can be a single entrée or a traditional churrasco. The latter is a variety of meats and sausages skewered on large "swords" that are brought to the table.

4 dried red chiles, stems and seeds removed, crushed
1 cup lemon juice, fresh preferred
1 large onion, chopped
1/2 cup fresh cilantro, or parsley, chopped
2 teaspoons salt
2 pounds tenderloin or flank steak

Combine all the ingredients and marinate the steak overnight. Remove the steak and grill until desired doneness is attained. Make a sauce by heating and thickening the marinade.

Serves: 4 to 6

Serving Suggestions: The sauce is spooned over the steak. In Brazil, a churrasco would be served with vegetables such as chopped greens, toasted manioc, and black beans, and accompanied by fresh orange slices.

Note: This recipe requires advance preparation.

HEAT SCALE: 3

Ecuadorean Pork Roast

This spiced roast is best served sliced and arranged on a platter, and then topped with the gravy. Serve with boiled potatoes and parslied buttered carrots or minted green peas. Accompany with a bowl of Chilean hot sauce (p. 96).

1 1/2 tablespoons crushed red chiles
4 cloves garlic
1/4 teaspoon saffron mixed with 1/4 cup hot water
1/2 teaspoon cumin seeds
1/2 teaspoon marjoram
1 teaspoon salt
1 teaspoon freshly ground pepper
4-pound pork loin roast
1/2 cup dry white wine
3 tablespoons red wine vinegar
1/2 cup onions, minced
2 tablespoons flour mixed with 2 tablespoons water

Make a paste of the chiles, garlic, saffron, cumin, marjoram, salt, and pepper. Rub the paste into the pork roast and marinate overnight in the refrigerator.

Place the meat in a roasting pan and place in a 425°F oven. Reduce the heat to 350°F, and cook for 2 hours or until the meat is done. Baste frequently with the drippings.

When done, remove the roast and skim the fat from the drippings. Add the wine, vinegar, and onion to the drippings, heat, and thicken with the flour.

Serves: 4 to 6
Note: This recipe requires advance preparation.
HEAT SCALE: 3

Orange Spiced Pork Chops

(COLUMBIA)

This dish resembles some Oriental sweet and sour recipes. The heat of the chiles is tempered by the sweetness and acidity of the oranges.

¹/₂ cup Chilean hot sauce (p. 96)
1 small onion, sliced and separated into rings
2 tablespoons butter
4 pork loin chops
1 tablespoon grated orange rind
¹/₂ cup orange juice
¹/₂ cup chicken stock
2 teaspoons cornstarch mixed with 1 tablespoon water

Sauté the onion in the butter until soft. Remove from the pan. Brown the pork chops in the pan on both sides, and top with the onions.

Mix together the orange rind, orange juice, stock, and hot sauce. Pour the sauce over the chops and simmer until the chops are tender, about 15 minutes. Remove the chops.

Thicken the sauce with the cornstarch mixture.

Serves: 4.
Serving Suggestions: Serve the chops with the onion rings topped with the thickened sauce and accompanied by a green vegetable and roasted or baked potatoes.

HEAT SCALE: 4

Bolivian Stuffed Chicken

An exotic chicken variation that makes an excellent main course for a festive occasion. For extra heat, serve accompanied by salsa boraccha (p. 55).

4 teaspoons dried ground red chile
1 roasting chicken
3 cloves garlic, whole
$1/2$ pound ground pork
1 cup cooked rice
1 small onion, chopped
$1/4$ cup tomato sauce
$1/2$ cup raisins
$1/2$ cup toasted almonds, chopped

Rub the chicken inside and out with the garlic. Mix together the remaining ingredients and stuff the chicken with the mixture.

Dot the chicken with butter and roast in a 350°F oven for 2 hours or until done. Baste frequently with the drippings.

Serves: 4 to 6
HEAT SCALE: 3

Peruvian Chicken in Nut Sauce

In this elegant dish, powerful heat is concealed within the walnut sauce.

3 santaka chiles, crushed, or 3 tablespoons red chile paste (p. 95)
3 fresh red or green chiles, skinned, seeds removed, cut into strips
4-pound chicken, quartered

4 cups chicken broth
2 cups fresh bread crumbs
2 cups milk
1 medium onion, chopped fine
3 cloves garlic, chopped fine
4 tablespoons oil
1 cup walnuts, ground
Salt and pepper to taste
1/4 cup grated white cheese
Hard-cooked egg slices for garnish

Cover the chicken with the broth and bring to a boil, skimming off any foam that forms. Reduce the heat and simmer until the chicken is tender but not falling off the bone. Remove the chicken, drain, and cool. Remove the skin from the chicken and shred the meat into pieces 2 inches long.

Cover the bread crumbs with 1 cup of the milk and let stand until the bread has absorbed the milk. Mash the bread to make a paste.

Sauté the onion and garlic in 2 tablespoons of the oil until soft. Add the santaka chiles (or red chile paste), walnuts, salt, and pepper and simmer for 5 minutes. Stir in the remaining oil and bread paste and stir until thoroughly mixed. Gradually add the remaining milk, stirring constantly, and heat until the sauce has thickened. Add the chicken and cheese and simmer until the chicken has heated and the cheese has melted. Garnish with the chile strips and eggs.

Serves: 4 to 6
Serving Suggestions: Serve with boiled potatoes or rice.
HEAT SCALE: 5

Pepper Shrimp

(BRAZIL)

Palm hearts add an authentic touch to this classic Brazilian
entrée. They are available in cans in most gourmet shops.

4 teaspoons crushed red chile
1 small onion, sliced thin
1 clove garlic, minced
1 bell pepper, julienne cut
2 tablespoons peanut oil
2 small tomatoes, peeled and chopped
3 teaspoons fresh parsley, chopped
1 teaspoon basil, crushed
1 1/2 pounds raw shrimp, peeled and deveined
1/4 cup flour
3 tablespoons butter
2 teaspoons cornstarch mixed with 2 teaspoons water
1 can palm hearts (any size)

Sauté the onion, garlic, and bell pepper in the oil until soft. Add
the crushed chile, tomatoes, parsley, and basil. Cover and
simmer 1/2 hour.

Dredge the shrimp in the flour. Sauté the shrimp in the
butter until golden brown.

Stir the cornstarch into the sauce and heat until it becomes
slightly thickened. Add the shrimp and palm hearts and heat for
5 minutes.

Serves: 6
Serving Suggestions: Serve over rice and accompany with
baked yams or sweet potatoes.
HEAT SCALE: 3

Vatapá de Camarao e Peixe

(BRAZIL)

Shrimp and fish in coconut-nut sauce is a classic Bahian dish that clearly illustrates the African influence in Brazil.

6 dried chile piquins, crushed, or 6 serrano chiles, chopped fine
1 teaspoon ground ginger
1 teaspoon paprika
2 pounds raw shrimp, peeled and deveined
2 pounds white fish fillets, cut in 2-inch pieces
4 tablespoons oil
1 small onion, chopped fine
2 medium tomatoes, peeled and chopped
1 1/2 cups milk
1 cup coconut milk (see p. 171)
1/2 cup ground roasted peanuts
1/2 cup ground cashew nuts
1/2 teaspoon coriander seeds
Salt and pepper to taste
2 tablespoons flour dissolved in 2 tablespoons cold water

Lightly brown the fish and shrimp in the oil, adding the shrimp a few at a time. Remove and drain. Add the onion and sauté until soft and transparent. Reduce the heat and add the chiles and tomatoes. Cover and cook over a medium heat for 10 minutes.

Stir in the milk, coconut milk, peanuts, cashews, coriander, salt, and pepper and simmer over low heat for 15 minutes. Stir in the flour mixture and cook until slightly thickened, stirring constantly. Puree the sauce until smooth. Return the sauce to the skillet and cook, stirring constantly until thick. Add the fish and shrimp and simmer until thoroughly heated.

Serves: 6
Serving Suggestions: Serve with or over rice, accompanied by slices of fresh orange, papaya, banana, pineapple, and mango and a green vegetable.
HEAT SCALE: 4

Fish Fillets in Coconut Milk

(COLUMBIA)

Coconuts are prevalent along the Caribbean coast of South America, so it's not surprising to see a fish dish with coconut milk here. Compare to recipes from Southeast Asia and the Pacific.

4 *fresh green chiles, skinned, seeds removed, chopped*
4 *white fish fillets, cut 1 inch thick*
2 *medium tomatoes, peeled and chopped*
1 *small onion, chopped*
2 *cups coconut milk (see p. 171)*
4 *tablespoons heavy cream*

Place the fish in a pan and cover with the chiles, tomatoes, onion, and coconut milk. Simmer for 10 minutes or until the fish is done. Remove the fish and keep warm.

Continue to simmer the sauce until it is reduced to 1 cup. Strain the sauce, stir in the cream, and heat until warm. Pour over the fish and serve.

Serves: 4
HEAT SCALE: 3

Chile Cheese Potatoes

(PERU)

The marinated onions provide the pungency in this dish, which utilizes a staple of the country, potatoes.

3 dried chile piquins
4 green chiles, skinned, seeds removed, chopped
1 green chile, skinned, seeds removed, cut in strips
1/2 cup lemon juice
1/4 teaspoon salt
1 large onion, sliced and separated into rings
2 cups Monterey Jack or cheddar cheese, grated
1 cup heavy cream
2 tablespoons olive oil
6 potatoes, boiled and diced

Mix the piquins, lemon juice, and salt. Add the onion rings and toss until coated. Cover and marinate, at room temperature, for 30 minutes. Drain.

Combine the cheese, cream, and chopped chile in a blender and puree until smooth. Heat the oil and slowly add the cheese mixture, stirring constantly. Simmer over a low heat until the sauce thickens, about 5 to 10 minutes.

To serve, pour the sauce over the hot potatoes and garnish with the drained onion rings and chile strips.

Serves: 4 to 6
HEAT SCALE: 5

Columbian Hot Squash

The presence of sugar in this vegetable casserole shows the influence of the Spanish—the tendency toward sweet dishes. This dish can be served as a side vegetable or as a luncheon entrée.

4 fresh red chiles, skinned, seeds removed, chopped fine or 4 dried
    red chiles that have been rehydrated
1 large onion, sliced and separated into rings
1 bell pepper, sliced
2 tablespoons butter
3 tablespoons flour
4 tablespoons brown sugar
4 tomatoes, peeled and quartered
Salt to taste
6 summer squashes, sliced
1 cup Monterey Jack cheese, grated

Sauté the onion rings and bell pepper in the butter until soft. Add the chiles and flour and cook until the flour begins to brown. Gradually add the brown sugar and cook over a low heat for 5 minutes. Place the tomato quarters over the mixture, salt to taste, and cook for an additional 10 minutes.

In a greased casserole, alternate layers of squash and tomato mixture. Top with the grated cheese and bake at 325°F for 35 to 40 minutes.

Serves: 6
HEAT SCALE: 3

Bolivian Baked Corn

Almost a soufflé, this corn casserole enhances any broiled or baked meat. It also makes a delicious buffet or brunch entrée.

3 teaspoons crushed red chile
1 tablespoon flour
1 tablespoon butter
1 pound whole kernel corn
2 eggs, beaten
1 cup Monterey Jack or Swiss cheese, grated

Sauté the flour and the chile in the butter. Combine the corn and eggs and add to the chile mixture, stirring well. Pour half the corn mixture into a greased casserole dish and cover with half the cheese. Add the remaining corn and top with the remaining cheese. Bake for 45 minutes to 1 hour at 350°F.

Serves: 4
HEAT SCALE: 4

8
Europe

Europeans prefer their hot food pungent rather than fiery, and that's the reason chiles are less common here than in other parts of the world. In fact, there are far more recipes containing mustard, horseradish, or large amounts of black pepper than chiles. On occasion hot chiles will surface in Spanish foods, but for the most part the only chile used extensively in Europe is paprika, which is generally about a 1 or 2 on the heat scale.

The paprika commonly sold in the United States lacks capsaicin and thus is mild and sweet. But in middle and southern European countries like Hungary, Romania, and Czechoslovakia, a more pungent paprika can be found. If you cannot locate an authentic hot paprika, a reasonable facsimile can be concocted by mixing three parts commercial paprika to one part hot ground chile powder. When using paprika, the consensus of chefs is to monitor the temperature of the cooking carefully, as overheating will break down the sugar content and spoil the flavor of paprika. In other words, don't boil paprika dishes, but rather simmer over very low heat.

Horseradish appears in most countries in the form of a sauce to be served with meat dishes or with salads, so we've included that recipe here. Mustard is loved in Europe and is also found most commonly in sauce form. Black or white pepper is a condiment in most main dishes, and occasionally becomes a truly pungent heat source, as in Steak aux Trois Poivres (p. 121).

Spiced Shrimp

(SPAIN)

The combined pungencies of mustard and horseradish result in a surprising seafood dish that would be served as a *tapa* or hors d'oeuvre at a streetside bar.

1 tablespoon prepared mustard, Dijon preferred
2 tablespoons horseradish sauce (see p. 115)
1 pound uncooked shrimp, shelled
1 tablespoon pickling spices
1–2 cups water
1/4 cup olive oil
4 green onions, chopped
1/2 teaspoon salt

Boil the shrimp in water containing the pickling spices until done, about 2 minutes. Drain the shrimp.

Combine all the other ingredients and toss the shrimp in the mixture until well coated. Marinate the shrimp overnight.

Serves: 4
Serving Suggestions: Serve on a bed of fresh spinach.
Note: This recipe requires advance preparation.
HEAT SCALE: 1

Russian Beet Salad

A sweetly pungent sauce accents the beets in this typical Russian salad or appetizer.

1 tablespoon horseradish, peeled and minced
6 medium beets, cooked and sliced
1 small onion, sliced and separated into rings
1/2 cup vinegar
1/4 cup water
4 tablespoons brown sugar
1/4 teaspoon caraway seeds
Salt to taste

Mix all the ingredients together and marinate overnight.

Serves: 4
Serving Suggestions: Before serving, garnish with fresh onion rings.
Note: This recipe requires advance preparation.
HEAT SCALE: 1

Spanish Pepper Salad

This recipe is unique because it contains four different varieties of Capsicum annuum used in diverse ways within the context of a single dish. The green or red chiles are used for taste and heat, the bell pepper just for taste, and the pimiento and paprika provide color as condiments and garnishes.

2 green or red chiles, skinned, seeds removed, chopped
1 1/2 teaspoons paprika
1 1/2 cups cooked rice
1 green or red bell pepper, sliced
2 tomatoes, peeled and chopped

1 tablespoon parsley, chopped
1/4 cup cooked peas
1/4 cup green olives, chopped
4 pimientos, cut in strips

DRESSING
1/4 teaspoon prepared mustard
6 tablespoons olive oil
2 tablespoons red wine vinegar
2 cloves garlic, crushed
Salt and ground black pepper to taste

Toss the rice with the dressing, add the remaining ingredients, except the pimiento, and marinate for 1 hour. Garnish with the pimientos and serve at room temperature.

Serves: 4
HEAT SCALE: 2

Onion Soup
(HUNGARY)

A soup similar to French onion, yet with a bite if made with hot paprika.

2 tablespoons Hungarian paprika
3 large onions, sliced and separated into rings
3 tablespoons butter
1 quart beef stock
3 tomatoes, peeled and chopped (optional)
1/4 teaspoon dried oregano, crushed
Salt

Sauté the onions in the butter until soft and browned. Add the paprika and fry, stirring constantly for 2 minutes. Add the remaining ingredients and simmer for 2 hours.

Serves: 4

Serving Suggestions: Excellent with a tossed green salad and dark rye bread for a light supper or hearty lunch.

HEAT SCALE: 2

Cream of Vegetable Soup

(HUNGARY)

Hungarians enjoy their vegetables in sauces or creams, as evidenced by this recipe. A variety of vegetables can be used, either in combination or as a single vegetable soup.

2 tablespoons Hungarian paprika
1 medium onion, chopped
2 stalks celery, chopped
1 quart chicken broth
1 pound vegetables, cut in pieces (asparagus, carrots, potatoes, green beans, etc.)
2 tablespoons flour
1/4 cup water
1/2 cup heavy cream
Salt and pepper to taste

Simmer the onion and celery in the broth until tender. Remove and puree in a blender or put through a sieve until smooth.

Return to the heat, add the vegetables, and simmer until the vegetables are tender, about 20 minutes.

Mix the flour and paprika with the water to make a paste and stir into the soup mixture. Heat until the soup thickens. Remove from the heat and slowly stir in the cream. Return to the heat and simmer for 10 minutes or until heated, being careful not to let it boil or the cream will curdle.

Serves: 4 to 6
HEAT SCALE: 2

Creamy Horseradish Sauce

(HUNGARY)

This is a basic sauce recipe that can be used in other recipes or as an accompaniment to plain meats such as prime rib or roast beef.

1/3 cup horseradish, peeled and grated
2 tablespoons butter or margarine
2 tablespoons flour
1/4 teaspoon salt
1/2 cup chicken broth
1 cup heavy cream

Melt the butter in a saucepan and stir in the flour and salt. Cook for two minutes, but do not allow the flour to brown. Stir in the broth and horseradish and heat. Slowly add the cream, stirring constantly. Cook until smooth and thickened.

Yield: 1 1/2 cups
HEAT SCALE: 2

Czechoslovakian Meatballs

These meatballs can be served as an entrée or, if made small, are good as hors d'oeuvres.

3 tablespoons Hungarian paprika
1 medium onion, chopped
2 cloves garlic, chopped
4 tablespoons butter
1 pound ground beef
1 egg, slightly beaten
1/2 cup soft bread crumbs
2 tablespoons flour
1 cup beef stock
1 cup sour cream
Salt and pepper to taste

Sauté the onion and garlic in 2 tablespoons of the butter until soft. Mix the onion, beef, egg, and bread crumbs together and shape into meatballs.

Fry the meatballs in the remaining butter until brown, remove and drain. Add the flour and paprika to the pan and lightly brown, stirring constantly. Add the stock to the flour mixture and bring to a boil. Reduce the heat and simmer until thickened. Stir in the sour cream and heat thoroughly. Return the meatballs and heat before serving.

Serves: 4 as an entrée
Serving Suggestions: Serve over noodles with a green vegetable for color.
HEAT SCALE: 2

Veal Paprikash with Spätzle

(HUNGARY)

Paprikash is a Hungarian classic combining paprika, two types of cream—sweet and sour—and a meat. We have included a recipe for spätzle, which is a variety of dumpling that is traditionally served with stews or soups.

3 tablespoons Hungarian paprika
1 large onion, chopped
1/2 cup bell pepper, chopped
1/4 cup olive oil
2 pounds veal, cubed
1/2 cup flour seasoned with salt and pepper
1/2 cup water
1 tablespoon butter
1/4 cup flour
1/2 cup light cream or half and half
1 cup sour cream
Freshly ground pepper to taste

Sauté the onion, bell pepper and 1 tablespoon of the paprika in the oil until the onions are lightly browned. Dredge the meat in flour seasoned with salt and pepper and add to the onions. Brown the meat on all sides. Add 1/2 the water and simmer until the meat is tender, stirring occasionally. Remove and drain.

Melt the butter, add the flour and the remaining paprika, and stir to make a smooth paste. Heat the mixture, stirring constantly, until it begins to bubble. Remove from the heat and slowly stir in the light cream.

Heat the sauce to just below boiling, stirring constantly. Remove from the heat and add the sour cream, a little at a time, stirring it into the sauce. Add the sauce and pepper to the meat, mix thoroughly, and simmer for 10 minutes.

SPÄTZLE
2 cups flour
1 egg, beaten
1 cup water
2 teaspoons salt

Mix all the ingredients together. Drop pea-size amounts of the dough into boiling salted water. Remove the spätzle when they surface.

Serves: 6
Serving Suggestions: Serve over noodles or spätzle.
HEAT SCALE: 2

Beef Goulash
(HUNGARY)

This dish can be a meal in itself—just add cooked potatoes and other vegetables before serving. It is simple to prepare and can be done in a crock pot.

3 tablespoons Hungarian paprika
1 pound chuck or flank steak, cubed
1/4 cup flour
3 tablespoons cooking oil
1 large onion, chopped
1 clove garlic, minced
1/4 cup mushrooms, sliced
2 cups beef broth
Salt to taste
1 cup white wine

Coat the beef cubes with the flour and brown in the oil. Remove the meat and place in a large saucepan or crock pot.

Sauté the onion and garlic until soft but not browned. Add the paprika and heat for an additional 2 minutes.

Combine all the ingredients with the meat, except for the wine, and simmer for 2 hours, stirring occasionally. Shortly before serving, add the wine.

Serves: 4

Serving Suggestions: Serve over wide noodles or with oven-browned potatoes and a green vegetable such as broccoli or green beans.

Variations: Just before serving, stir in 1 cup of sour cream; this is a Western adaptation, but still good. For more heat, add cayenne powder.

HEAT SCALE: 2

Fondue Bourguignonne
(SWITZERLAND)

Although not the traditional fondue, which is cheese, this recipe is fun, especially when you experiment with your own sauce variations. With this dish, each individual uses a fondue fork to fry the steak cubes in the oil. The sauces are used for dipping according to taste and desired pungency.

½ pound top sirloin steak per person, cut in 1-inch cubes
Garlic salt
Peanut oil
¼ pound butter

Season beef cubes with the garlic salt. Heat the peanut oil until nearly smoking, add the butter, and cover. When ready to eat, transfer the oil to a fondue pot. After cooking the steak, dip in one of the following sauces.

CURRIED MAYONNAISE
3/4 tablespoon curry powder
2 hard-cooked eggs, chopped fine
1/4 teaspoon dry mustard
3/4 cup mayonnaise
1 teaspoon lemon juice
Salt to taste

Combine all the ingredients and let sit for 20 minutes to blend the flavors.

Yield: 3/4 cup
HEAT SCALE: 1

MUSTARD SAUCE
1 tablespoon dry mustard
2 tablespoons prepared mustard
2 tablespoons cider vinegar
3/4 cup mayonnaise

Combine all the ingredients and let sit for 20 minutes to blend the flavors.

Yield: 3/4 cup
HEAT SCALE: 1

HORSERADISH SAUCE
2 tablespoons horseradish, peeled and grated
2 tablespoons chives, chopped
1 teaspoon lemon juice
1 cup sour cream
Salt to taste

Combine all ingredients.

Yield: 1 cup
HEAT SCALE: 1

CURRY SAUCE
3 teaspoons curry powder
¹/₂ teaspoon powdered ginger
¹/₂ cup onion, chopped
¹/₂ cup celery, chopped
2 tablespoons butter
2 tablespoons flour
2 cups chicken broth

Sauté onion and celery in the butter until tender. Stir in ginger, curry, and flour and heat for 2 minutes. Add the stock, stirring constantly, until the mixture thickens. Cook over a low heat for 5 minutes. Remove and serve.

Yield: 2¹/₂ cups
HEAT SCALE: 2

Steak aux Trois Poivres

(FRANCE)

This amazing dish violates at least two laws Americans have about steak: never season heavily and never fry in a pan. But the taste of this peppered steak is so good, we'll forget the rules. Three different varieties of pepper are recommended, but it is excellent with just crushed black peppercorns.

2 tablespoons black peppercorns, crushed*
1 tablespoon white pepper powder
1 tablespoon green peppercorns, crushed*
1 teaspoon Tabasco sauce (optional)
1 teaspoon salt
4 filets or New York strip steaks at least 1 inch thick
4 tablespoons butter
¹/₄ cup Worcestershire sauce
¹/₄ cup brandy

Coat both sides of the steaks with the crushed peppercorns, the white pepper, and the green peppercorns. Press the pepper into the steak with a blunt instrument and leave the steaks out, uncovered, at room temperature for at least 1 hour.

Sprinkle salt in a large skillet and heat very hot, until the salt begins to turn brown. Sear the steaks on each side quickly. Add the butter and cook the steaks for 1 minute on each side. Add the Worcestershire sauce and the Tabasco sauce and cook another 1 to 3 minutes per side, depending upon the thickness of the steaks and degree of doneness desired. Pour the brandy over the steaks, wait 10 seconds, then set aflame. When the flame goes out, remove the steaks to a serving platter. Reduce the remaining liquid in the pan and serve over the steaks. The steaks should be rare.

Serves: 4

Serving Suggestions: This steak dish is excellent with a fresh spinach salad and twice-baked potatoes.

Variation: For a heavier sauce, add 1/4 cup cream after removing the steaks.

Note: This recipe requires advance preparation.

HEAT SCALE: 2

*Wrap the peppercorns in a cloth and crush them with a pestle or hammer. Grinding them in a peppermill makes the pepper too fine.

Rabbit with Mustard

(FRANCE)

This elegant dish combines the world-famous French mustard with a rich, creamy wine sauce.

2 tablespoons Dijon mustard
4 boneless rabbit thighs
¹/₂ cup butter
2 cups chicken broth
1 cup white wine
2 tablespoons flour
Salt to taste
1 cup light cream
¹/₂ cup grated Parmesan cheese

Sauté the rabbit thighs in half the butter in a frying pan until lightly browned. Mix the broth and wine, add to the rabbit, cover, and simmer the rabbit until tender, about an hour. Remove the rabbit and place in a baking pan.

Melt the remaining butter in a saucepan, add the flour and salt, sauté for a couple of minutes, but do not let the flour brown. Stir in the cream and mustard and cook over a low heat until thick.

Spread sauce over the rabbit and top with the grated cheese. Place under the broiler until the cheese begins to brown.

Serves: 4
Serving Suggestions: Serve with asparagus spears or sautéed mushrooms and duchess potatoes.
Variation: Substitute chicken breasts for the rabbit.
HEAT SCALE: 1

Paprikash Chicken
(HUNGARY)

A variation of the classic paprikash dish, which requires more preparation time.

4 tablespoons Hungarian paprika
4-pound chicken
2 tablespoons butter
1 large onion, thinly sliced and separated into rings
2 tablespoons flour
1 cup dry white wine
1 cup chicken stock
1 cup sour cream
Salt and pepper to taste

Rub the chicken with 2 tablespoons of the paprika and set aside for 2 to 3 hours.

Melt the butter. Place the chicken on a rack in a casserole, baste with half the butter, and cover with the onions. Place in a 450°F oven and immediately reduce the heat to 350°F. Roast until the chicken is done, about 1 to 1½ hours, basting frequently.

Remove the chicken and add the remaining butter to the drippings. Stir in the flour and remaining paprika and cook for 2 to 3 minutes. Add the wine and stock, bring to a boil, immediately reduce the heat, and simmer until the mixture thickens. Slowly add the sour cream, stirring constantly, until heated.

Return the chicken to the casserole, cover with the sauce, add salt and pepper to taste, and serve.

Serves: 4 to 6
Serving Suggestions: Serve with hot buttered noodles and broccoli or peas.
Note: This recipe requires advance preparation.
HEAT SCALE: 2

Romanian Chicken Livers

The Hungarian influence is very evident in this dish. Serve the livers over or with rice and with the traditional roasted and marinated sweet bell peppers.

1 1/2 tablespoons Hungarian paprika
1 small onion, chopped
1 clove garlic, minced
6 tablespoons butter
1 cup sliced mushrooms
1 pound chicken livers
2 tablespoons flour
1/2 cup chicken broth
1/4 cup dry red wine or sherry
1/2 cup sour cream

Sauté the onion and garlic in 4 tablespoons of the butter until soft. Add the mushrooms and sauté for an additional 2 to 3 minutes. Remove the onion, garlic, and mushrooms from the pan.

Sauté the chicken livers in the pan, adding the rest of the butter if necessary. Mix the flour and paprika and add to the livers so as to cover each piece.

Add the broth and simmer until the livers are done, about 15 minutes. Reduce the heat and return the onion, garlic, and mushrooms to the pan. Stir in the wine and sour cream, taking care not to let the mixture boil.

Serves: 4
HEAT SCALE: 1

Baked Fish with Mustard Sauce
(YUGOSLAVIA)

This simple, easy to prepare fish entrée goes well with a rice pilaf and minted carrots.

1 pound baked white fish fillets (sole, flounder, cod)

SAUCE
1 tablespoon dry mustard mixed with 1 tablespoon water
2 tablespoons butter
2 tablespoons flour
¹/4 teaspoon salt
1 cup chicken broth
Caraway seeds

Melt the butter and stir in the flour and salt. Heat over a low heat until the flour is lightly browned. Mix the mustard and the broth and slowly add to the flour mixture. Simmer, stirring constantly, until thick.

Pour over baked fish fillets, garnish with the caraway seeds, and serve.

Serves: 4
HEAT SCALE: 1

Salmon with Horseradish

(GERMANY)

Horseradish is the most common pungent ingredient used in the cooking of northern Europe.

2 tablespoons fresh horseradish, peeled and grated
1 potato, peeled and chopped
1 small onion, chopped
1 carrot, peeled and diced
2 cups water
2 tablespoons flour
1/2 teaspoon salt
2 tablespoons butter
1 cup light cream
4 salmon fillets

Simmer the vegetables in the water until very soft. Remove and save the liquid.

Sauté the flour and salt in the butter for a couple of minutes, taking care not to let the flour brown. Mix the cream and the vegetable water and stir into the flour mixture. Bring this sauce to a boil, add the fish, reduce the heat, and simmer until the fish is done, about 15 minutes.

Remove the fish and spread the horseradish over it. Pour the sauce over the fish and serve at once.

Serves: 4
Serving Suggestions: Serve with hot potato salad and asparagus spears.
HEAT SCALE: 2

Spaghetti Carbonara

(ITALY)

The trick to this "Roman" dish is to organize all the ingredients and keep them hot. The heat of the ingredients will cook the raw eggs and make the sauce.

1 tablespoon red pepper flakes or crushed red chile pods
1/4 cup butter
2 whole eggs
1 cup freshly grated Parmesan cheese
10 slices bacon
1/2 pound spaghetti

Cream the butter and set aside. Beat together the eggs and half the cheese. Set aside.

Cook the bacon until crisp, remove from pan, drain, and crumble. Pour off the bacon fat until 4 tablespoons remain. Add the red pepper flakes and heat in the bacon fat.

Cook the spaghetti, drain quickly, and place in a warm serving bowl. Add the butter and toss. Next, pour the bacon fat and pepper mixture over the spaghetti and toss until coated. Then add the egg mixture and quickly toss until thoroughly mixed. Top with the crumbled bacon, remaining cheese, and serve at once.

Serves: 2 as an entrée, 4 as an accompanying dish.

Serving Suggestions: A "typical" Italian meal of tossed green salad and garlic bread goes well with this pasta dish.

Variation: For a creamier sauce, slowly stir in 1/2 cup heavy cream to the bacon fat/pepper mixture.

HEAT SCALE: 3

Cheese Fondue

(SWITZERLAND)

We have added Tabasco to this traditional Swiss dish. To connoisseurs, the best part of this fondue is the thick residue at the
bottom of the pot.

1 teaspoon Tabasco sauce
1/2 teaspoon paprika
4 teaspoons mustard powder
4 tablespoons butter
4 tablespoons flour
Salt to taste
1 cup beer
1 cup milk
1 pound Gruyère cheese
1 loaf of day-old French bread, cut into cubes

Melt the butter in a saucepan, stir in the flour and salt, and heat
for 2 minutes. Stir in the beer and milk and simmer gently until
slightly thickened. Stir in the Tabasco sauce, paprika, and
mustard. Gradually add the cheese, stirring constantly until it
melts, taking care not to let it boil. Transfer to a fondue dish and
dip the bread cubes, skewered on fondue forks, into the fondue.

Yield: 4 cups
HEAT SCALE: 2

Hungarian Baked Potatoes

These potatoes add color as well as a little spice to a meal.

2 tablespoons Hungarian paprika
1 large onion, chopped
1 tablespoon oil
4 potatoes, baked in their skins
4 tablespoons butter
3 tablespoons milk or cream

Sauté the onion in the oil until soft. Add the paprika and fry until the onion is golden brown.

Remove the potatoes from their skins and save the skins. Mash the potatoes with the butter and milk and mix in the onion mixture. Re-stuff the skins with the potato mixture, then heat and serve.

Serves: 4
HEAT SCALE: 2

Dilled Zucchini

(YUGOSLAVIA)

This dish can be served hot as a vegetable dish or cold as a salad or relish.

1 tablespoon Hungarian paprika
1 medium onion, chopped
2 tablespoons oil
1 pound zucchini, sliced
1 teaspoon dill seeds
$^1/_2$ cup sour cream

Sauté the onion in the oil until soft. Add the zucchini and dill. Cover and cook over low heat until the zucchini is done but still crisp.

Mix the paprika and sour cream. Stir into the zucchini mixture. Heat and serve.

Serves: 4
Serving Suggestions: Good with roast beef.
HEAT SCALE: 1

9
Africa and the Middle East

The hot foods of this part of the world are based mostly upon chiles, though ginger and black pepper are also sometimes used. Chile usage is as common here as in Mexico, but sauces are not used as often and the smaller chiles like santakas and piquins appear whole in main dishes. Africans love their chiles as hot as possible, as can be seen by the varieties that appear in their recipes. Cayenne is perhaps the chile cultivated most extensively in Africa, and it is utilized in the super-hot curries that Africans borrowed from the Indian immigrants. Like that of South America, African cooking has resulted from a collision of cultures. One of the more interesting food combinations found in Africa is chiles and peanuts, which appears commonly in west and central African foods. The taste, though as foreign to North American palates as the Mexican combination of chile and chocolate, is equally wonderful.

In the Middle East, curries are the principal source of heat, though santakas and piquins sometimes appear in the salads of Israel and Lebanon.

Falafel

(ISRAEL)

Falafels are served as appetizers or can be used as a sandwich filling. They are popular served in pita bread "pockets" with onions, lettuce, and tomatoes.

6 teaspoons dried red chile, crushed
4 cups cooked chick-peas
1 large onion, chopped
1 tablespoon parsley, chopped
1/4 teaspoon garlic powder
1 teaspoon ground cumin
1/4 cup cracker crumbs
2 eggs
1 cup bread crumbs
Oil for frying

Place the chile, chick-peas, onion, parsley and spices, cracker crumbs, and eggs in a blender and puree until smooth. Form the mixture into balls and roll in the bread crumbs. Flatten them slightly to form "fingers."

Deep-fry these fingers in the hot oil until browned on all sides. Remove and drain.

Yield: 3 dozen
HEAT SCALE: 3

Salata Mechioua
Tunisian Grilled Salad

In Tunisia, this is served as a summer salad or dip. Traditionally it is prepared outside over clay charcoal braziers and pulverized in brass mortars. It is impressive at a barbecue when made in front of guests.

> 6 *fresh green or red chiles*
> 2 *medium onions*
> 3 *cloves garlic*
> 4 *tomatoes*

Do not skin or peel any of the vegetables but place all the ingredients whole over charcoal or under a broiler, turning occasionally. Grill the vegetables until the skins pop and burn. Remove from heat and peel all the vegetables. Pulverize or puree to a coarse sauce.

Serves: 4
Serving Suggestions: Serve with a loaf of French bread. Tear off pieces of bread and dip them in the sauce.
HEAT SCALE: 4

Avocado and Chile Salad
(ISRAEL)

An unusual salad that combines fruit, vegetables, and two kinds of heat.

> 2 *teaspoons crushed red chile*
> 1/2 *teaspoon fresh ginger, grated*
> 2 *tablespoons raisins*
> 1/4 *cup warm water*

1 cup orange juice
Salt to taste
1 1/2 cups carrots, grated
2 avocados, peeled and cut into wedges

Soak the raisins in water for 30 minutes, then drain.

Combine the chile, ginger, orange juice, and salt. Add the carrots and toss until they are well coated. Marinate the mixture for 2 hours in the refrigerator.

Arrange the avocado on a plate, top with the marinated carrots, and garnish with the raisins.

Serves: 4
Note: This recipe requires advance preparation.
HEAT SCALE: 3

Ethiopian Lentil Salad

Ethiopia has been a Christian country since around A.D. 300. This lentil salad is traditionally served on the meatless days during Lent.

6 fresh red or green chiles, skinned, seeds removed, cut in thin
strips
3 tablespoons red wine vinegar
1 clove garlic, minced
3 tablespoons oil
Salt and papper to taste
2 cups cooked lentils
8 large green onions, chopped (including greens)

Combine the vinegar, garlic, oil, salt, and pepper. Heat to just below boiling and cool to room temperature. Let stand for 1 hour and strain.

Add the lentils, onions, and chiles to the dressing, toss well, and marinate at room temperature for at least 2 hours before serving.

Serves: 4 to 6
Note: This recipe requires advance preparation.
HEAT SCALE: 4

Tunisian Shourba

Hot Soup

Serve this soup with crusty French bread and a crisp garden salad for a hearty lunch.

4 teaspoons red chile, crushed
1 1/2 pounds beef, cut in 1/2-inch cubes
1 large onion, chopped fine
1/4 cup olive oil
2 tablespoons tomato paste
3 cups beef broth
Salt to taste
1/2 cup pasta (noodles, macaroni, or vermicelli)
3 tablespoons fresh parsley, chopped
1 1/2 teaspoons lemon juice

Sauté the meat and onion in the oil for 5 minutes, stirring frequently. Add the tomato paste, chile, broth and salt, cover, and simmer for 1 hour. Add pasta and additional water, if necessary, and cook until the pasta is tender.

Before serving, add the parsley and lemon juice.

Serves: 4 to 6
HEAT SCALE: 3

Nigerian Groundnut Soup

Peanuts are a large cash crop in Nigeria, where they are called groundnuts. This recipe is an unusual combination of peanut butter and chiles made into a soup.

2 santaka chiles or 6 chile piquins, whole
3 cups chicken broth
2 carrots, diced
1 medium onion, chopped
Salt to taste
1 cup smooth peanut butter

Combine the broth, carrots, and onion in a saucepan and bring to a boil. Reduce the heat and simmer, partially covered, for an hour.

Puree the soup in a blender until smoth and then return to the pan. Bring the soup to a boil, add the chiles and salt, cover, and simmer for 40 minutes.

Mix the peanut butter with ½ cup of the soup until smooth. Stir this mixture into the soup and simmer for 10 minutes. Remove the chiles and serve.

Serves: 4
HEAT SCALE: 4

Berberé
Ethiopian Red Chile Paste

This exotic and fiery hot paste is a currylike variant of similar recipes from Latin America (see p. 95) and Southeast Asia (p. 177). It can be used in recipes from Africa and the Middle East where a strong heat source is needed.

1/2 cup red chile powder
1 teaspoon ground ginger
1/4 cup onion, chopped
3 cloves garlic
2 tablespoons oil
1/2 teaspoon each ground cardamon, cloves, allspice, nutmeg,
  cinnamon
2 tablespoons flour
1 cup water

Sauté the onion and garlic in the oil until soft and then mash them in the pan with a fork. Add the chile powder, spices, and flour. Sauté the mixture over a low heat until it is thoroughly mixed and heated, adding more oil if necessary. Slowly add the water and blend until a very thick sauce or paste forms.

Yield: 1 cup
Serving Suggestions: Serve with kitfo, which is raw minced beef mixed with chopped raw onions and spices. The raw meat is dipped in the berberé and eaten. Berberé can also be used as a dip or a sauce for cooked meats such as chicken or beef.

HEAT SCALE: 8

South African Peach Chutney

Chutneys, like relishes, are served as a accompaniment to meat and fowl dishes. Apparently of Indian origin, many different variations appear from former British colonies, often as part of curry dishes. Not all have this firepower, but many, like the dish below, combine fruit and the pungency of small, hot chiles.

4 chiles piquins, crumbled
1 1-inch piece fresh ginger, peeled and minced
2 cups dried peaches, chopped
2 tablespoons sugar
3/4 cup vinegar
1 large onion, chopped
2 cloves garlic, minced
2 cups water
1 cup blanched almonds, crushed
2 teaspoons ground coriander

Combine the peaches, sugar, vinegar, onion, garlic, and water in a pan and bring to a boil, stirring constantly. Reduce the heat and simmer for 30 minutes or until the mixture is thick and the peaches are soft. Place the peach mixture in a blender and puree with the almonds, coriander, chile, and ginger until smooth.

Cool to room temperature before serving. This chutney will keep for a month, covered, in the refrigerator.

Yield: 2½ to 3 cups.
Variation: Substitute apricots for the peaches.
HEAT SCALE: 4

Chakchouka

(TUNISIA)

This traditional Tunisian dish could more aptly be called a vegetable hash. It makes an excellent luncheon dish.

4 green chiles, skinned, seeds removed, cut in strips
2 serrano chiles, chopped fine
2 large onions, sliced in thin wedges
3 tablespoons olive oil
4 large tomatoes, peeled and diced
1 bell pepper, chopped
1 tablespoon vinegar
Salt
4 eggs

Sauté the onion in the oil until transparent. Add all the other ingredients except the eggs. Simmer this mixture, covered, until the vegetables are very soft.

Make 4 indentations in the vegetables and carefully break an egg into each one. Cover the pan and cook over a low heat until the eggs are well set.

Serves: 4
HEAT SCALE: 4

Beef and Peppers

(ETHIOPIA)

Serve this dish with a bowl of Ethiopian berberé (p. 138) on the side. Guests can then adjust the pungency according to individual taste.

6–7 green chiles, skinned, seeds removed, chopped
2 teaspoons fresh ginger, peeled and chopped
4 cloves garlic, chopped
1/4 teaspoon each ground cardamon, turmeric, cinnamon, cloves
1/2 cup red wine
2 pounds sirloin steak, cut in 1/2-inch-thick strips
6 tablespoons oil
2 cups onion, chopped
2 bell peppers, cut into strips

Puree the chiles, ginger, garlic, spices, and wine to a smooth paste.

Brown the beef in the hot oil. When evenly browned, remove and drain off all but 2 tablespoons of oil. Sauté the onion in the oil until soft but not browned. Add the bell peppers and sauté for an additional 3 minutes. Add the chile puree and bring to a boil, stirring constantly. Add the beef and mix until the strips are coated with the sauce. Reduce the heat and simmer for 10 minutes or more until the beef is done.

Serves: 6
Serving Suggestions: Serve with rice or boiled potatoes and sliced carrots.
HEAT SCALE: 4

Moroccan Brochettes

Moroccans love to cook outdoors over charcoal braziers. Roadside stands selling various kinds of broiled meat and crusty flat bread are quite common throughout the country.

4 teaspoons red chile powder
2 pounds ground beef
2 tablespoons fresh parsley, chopped fine
1 medium onion, chopped fine
1/2 teaspoon powdered cumin
1 teaspoon dried oregano, crushed
Salt and pepper to taste

Mix all ingredients together. Shape into 2-inch balls and place on wooden skewers (which have been soaked in water.) Broil the brochettes over charcoal until done.

Serves: 4 to 6
Serving Suggestions: Serve over rice or with couscous or in bread as a sandwich.
HEAT SCALE: 3

Nigerian Beef Kabobs

The heat of these kabobs is controlled by the amount and type of chile used—traditionally they are very, very hot.

2/3 cup crushed red chile
1 1/2 pounds beef, cut in 2-inch cubes
12 ounces beer
1 1/2 cups crushed peanuts

Marinate the beef in the beer for 3 or 4 hours.

Roll the beef cubes in a mixture of the peanuts and chile until they are completely covered. Put the cubes on skewers and grill over charcoal until done.

Serves: 4 to 6
Serving Suggestions: A cucumber salad and glazed carrots go well with this summer dish, but in Nigeria they are eaten right off the grill as an appetizer.
Note: This recipe calls for advance preparation.
HEAT SCALE: 8

Lamb in Peanut Sauce

(NIGERIA)

Peanut butter and chile sauces are common in many of the West African stews. The sauce used in this recipe is very versatile and can be used over many kinds of meat and poultry.

2 teaspoons dried santaka chile, crushed
1 pound lamb, cut in 1-inch cubes
3 tablespoons oil
Water
1/4 cup raw peanuts
1/2 cup peanut butter
1/4 teaspoon nutmeg
Salt to taste
Shredded coconut for garnish

Sauté the lamb cubes in 2 tablespoons of the oil until browned. Barely cover with water, cover, and simmer for 1 hour or until lamb is tender. Drain.

Sauté the peanuts and chile in the remaining oil for five minutes. Add the peanut butter and mix thoroughly. Stir in 1/2 cup water, nutmeg, and salt to taste, to the peanut sauce. Add the lamb, cover, and simmer until heated. Garnish with the coconut.

Serves: 4
Serving Suggestions: Serve over rice. Accompany with hard-cooked egg slices and fresh pineapple and papaya.
HEAT SCALE: 6

Lamb Tajine

(TUNISIA)

A tajine is both a stew and the name of the clay pot in which it is cooked. Many combinations of meats, vegetables, and even fruits are used in tajine.

5 green chiles, skinned, seeds removed, cut in strips
1 pound boneless lamb, cubed
1 large onion, chopped
2 tablespoons oil
Water
Salt to taste
2 unpeeled potatoes, diced
2 tomatoes, peeled and chopped
1 cup stuffed green olives

Sauté the lamb and onion until the meat is browned. Barely cover with water, salt to taste, cover and simmer for 1 hour or until the meat is tender. Add the vegetables, cover, and simmer until done—about 30 minutes.

Serves: 4
Serving Suggestions: Serve the tajine over couscous and with French bread.
HEAT SCALE: 4

Braised Chicken with Chiles

(GHANA)

Fresh tropical fruits such as pineapple, papaya, or mango along with baked yams will complement this easily prepared chicken.

3–4 green chiles, skinned, seeds removed, chopped
1 3-pound chicken, cut into 8 or 10 pieces
2 tablespoons butter
1 tablespoon peanut oil
1 onion, sliced and separated into rings
1 cup chicken broth
$^1/_2$ teaspoon ground nutmeg
Salt and pepper to taste

Melt the butter and oil and brown the chicken, a few pieces at a time. As the chicken browns, remove and keep warm. Add the onion rings and sauté until soft.

Add the broth, nutmeg, salt, pepper, and chile and bring to a boil. Put the chicken back in the pan, cover with the stock, reduce the heat, and simmer until the chicken is done—about 45 minutes.

Serves: 4
Variation: Make a stew by adding coarsely chopped onions, tomatoes, and corn while the chicken is simmering.
HEAT SCALE: 3

Galinha Muamba

Angolan Chicken

A number of vegetables can be added to "Angola's National Dish," including chopped carrots, pumpkin, squash, potatoes, or even turnips. Add them when you brown the solids from the marinade, adjust the water, and proceed with the recipe.

3–4 fresh red or green chiles, skinned, seeds removed, chopped
    fine
1/2 teaspoon ground ginger
1 large onion, chopped fine
3 cloves garlic, chopped fine
Salt and pepper to taste
1 cup lemon juice
2 cups water
6 tablespoons oil
1 3-pound chicken, cut in pieces

Combine the chiles, ginger, onion, garlic, salt, pepper, lemon juice, 1 cup of the water, oil and mix well. Place the chicken pieces in the mixture and marinate, at room temperature, for 3 hours. Remove the chicken and pat dry. Strain the marinade and reserve both the liquids and the solids.

Brown the chicken pieces in the remaining oil, removing them as they become browned. Add more oil if needed. Add the solids from the marinade and cook until the onions are soft but not browned. Return the chicken to the pan and add 1/2 cup of the marinade and the remaining 1 cup of water. Cover partially and simmer over low heat for 30 minutes or until the chicken is tender.

Serves: 4 to 6
Note: This recipe requires advance preparation.
HEAT SCALE: 3

Orange Chicken

(ISRAEL)

This is one of the milder recipes in this book—but also one of the tastiest. If possible, use Jaffa oranges, which are flavorful, thick-skinned oranges from Israel.

2 teaspoons fresh ginger, peeled and minced
1 cup orange juice (fresh preferred)
1 teaspoon grated orange rind
1/4 cup Cointreau
1 4-pound chicken
4 – 6 tablespoons honey
1/2 cup white wine
Salt to taste
1/4 cup flour mixed with 1/4 cup water

Mix the ginger, orange juice, orange rind, and Cointreau together. Place the chicken, breast side down, in a roasting pan. Pour the orange juice sauce over the chicken and bake, uncovered, at 350°F for 30 minutes.

Remove the chicken and baste the breast of the chicken with honey. Return to the pan breast side up and bake 10 more minutes. Then pour the white wine over the top of the chicken. Continue baking the chicken, basting frequently with the drippings, for about 1 hour.

Remove the chicken from the pan and keep warm. Heat the drippings until boiling and slowly stir in the flour mixture. Continue to stir until the sauce thickens.

Serves: 4
Serving Suggestions: Carve the chicken, then pour the sauce over the slices and serve the excess sauce in a side dish. Garnish with fresh orange slices and serve with rice and green peas.

HEAT SCALE: 1

Mozambique Camarao Piripiri

Spicy Shrimp

In Africa, "piripiri" is used to describe the chiles as well as dishes that contain them.

4 tablespoons crushed red chile
4 cloves garlic, chopped
1 1/2 cups oil (peanut preferred)
Salt to taste
2 pounds jumbo shrimp, peeled and deveined
4 tablespoons butter
1/2 cup fresh lemon juice

Combine the garlic, and 1/2 cup of the oil in a blender and puree until smooth. Add the chile, remaining oil, salt, and shrimp and toss until the shrimp is completely covered. Marinate the shrimp in the refrigerator for 4 hours.

Broil the shrimp over charcoal or under a broiler. Melt the butter and stir in the lemon juice. Add 1/2 cup marinade to the lemon oil. To serve, pour the lemon/pepper butter over the shrimp.

Serves: 4 to 6
Note: This recipe requires advance preparation.
HEAT SCALE: 6

Spicy Carrots
(TUNISIA)

Hirsa, which is a mixture of chile, cumin, and salt, is what gives these carrots their "spice." This dish is served both hot as a vegetable dish and cold as a salad.

2 teaspoons red chile powder
1 pound carrots, cut julienne
Water
Salt to taste
2 tablespoons olive oil
1 tablespoon vinegar
$1/2$ teaspoon cumin seed

Simmer the carrots in the water and salt until just tender. Remove from pan and drain. Toss the carrots in a mixture of the oil and vinegar. Add the remaining ingredients and heat until warm.

Serves: 4 to 6
Variation: Serve cold as a salad.
HEAT SCALE: 3

Ethiopian Ginger Vegetables

This casserole can be served as a vegetarian entrée as well as a vegetable side dish.

5 green chiles, skinned, seeds removed, chopped
1 teaspoon fresh ginger, grated
6 small potatoes, cubed
1/2 pound green beans
4 carrots, cut into strips
Water
2 medium onions, quartered and separated
2 tablespoons olive oil
2 cloves garlic, minced
Salt and pepper to taste

Place the potatoes, green beans, and carrots into boiling salted water to cover and cook for 5 minutes. Remove the vegetables and rinse.

Sauté the chile and onion in oil until soft but not browned. Add the ginger, garlic, salt, and pepper and sauté for 5 minutes. Add the rest of the ingredients, stir well, and cook over medium heat until the vegetables are tender but still fairly crisp.

Serves: 6
HEAT SCALE: 4

10
The Indian Subcontinent

Everyone knows that India is famous for its hot dishes called curries, so they rush out to buy curry powder when they wish to be authentic in serving Indian food. In India, however, cooks rarely use a standardized curry powder; they prefer to season each dish individually. Lamb, for example, requires a different combination of spices from fish. For Americans, such conventions may be difficult to follow because of the lack of availability of fresh spices. We've included an excellent recipe for a standard curry powder (p. 19) in the chapter Pungent Preparations, which should cover nearly all the curry recipes. The exceptions are curry dishes that individually list the different spices in curry powder as separate ingredients.

It seems that every spice in the known universe is included in curry powders, but the ingredients that make it pungent are the chiles—usually cayenne or ground santakas—and ground mustard seed. In addition to curries, many Indian dishes contain extra mustard. Ginger is also a common pungent ingredient in Indian cooking.

Cucumbers and Yoghurt

(INDIA)

There are a wide variety of yoghurt-based salads or relishes, called *raytas*, in India. They combine spices, yoghurt, and a variety of vegetables both raw and cooked. This one utilizes cucumbers and tomatoes.

3 green chiles, skinned, seeds removed, chopped
1/2 cup plain yoghurt
1/2 cup sour cream
2 tablespoons fresh mint, chopped
1/2 teaspoon ground cumin
3 medium cucumbers, peeled and thinly sliced
2 small tomatoes, diced

Combine the yoghurt, sour cream, mint, and cumin to form the dressing. Mix the vegetables together, pour the dressing over the top, and toss gently. Marinate in the refrigerator for 2 hours before serving.

Serves: 4 to 6
Note: This recipe requires advance preparation.
HEAT SCALE: 3

Cold Curry Dressing

(INDIA)

This dressing is especially good to top chicken or fish salads. It combines pungency with cool temperatures.

3 teaspoons curry powder (p. 19)
1 teaspoon prepared mustard
2 tablespoons sugar
1 egg, beaten
2 tablespoons butter
2 tablespoons flour
1 cup milk
¹/₄ cup vinegar
Salt

Combine the curry powder, mustard, and sugar. Add the egg and stir until smooth.

Melt the butter and stir in the flour. Heat for 2 minutes, stirring constantly. Add the milk and curry mixture. Cook the mixture until thickened, stirring constantly. Slowly add the vinegar, salt to taste, mix, and refrigerate before serving.

Yield: 1¹/₄ cups
Serving Suggestions: Serve cold over meats or raw vegetables.
HEAT SCALE: 2

Mulligatawny Soup

(INDIA)

Exactly where this soup originated is unclear, but it is believed to have been developed by Indian cooks for their British employers during colonial times. There are many variations, but all start with a spicy broth.

1½–2 tablespoons curry powder (p. 19)
1 cup onion, diced
2 cloves garlic, minced
1 cup celery, diced
1 cup carrots, diced
¼ cup butter
4 tablespoons flour
6 cups chicken broth
2 cups cooked chicken, diced
½ cup tart apples, diced
1 cup cooked rice
Salt to taste

Sauté the onion, garlic, and vegetables in the butter until soft. Add the curry and flour and heat, stirring constantly to avoid lumping. Add the broth and simmer for 20 minutes. Add the chicken, apples, rice, and salt. Cover and simmer for an additional 15 to 20 minutes.

Serves: 6 to 8
Variations: Stir in ½ cup warm cream before serving. Puree the vegetables or strain the broth before adding the chicken and rice, and serve with the cream.
HEAT SCALE: 2

Indian Split Pea Soup

This vegetarian soup is a curry-type variation on an old favorite.

3 teaspoons chile powder
1/2 teaspoon powdered ginger
2 cups split peas
3/4 teaspoon powdered turmeric
1 teaspoon powdered coriander
1 quart water or chicken broth
1 cup green onions, chopped (including greens)
2 tomatoes, diced
1 teaspoon toasted cumin seeds, crushed
Salt to taste

Wash the split peas and soak overnight.

Add the split peas, chile, ginger, turmeric, and coriander to the broth. Bring to a boil, reduce the heat, and simmer until the peas are done, about 2 hours. Remove from the heat and puree until smooth.

Add the remaining ingredients to the puree and simmer for an additional 20 minutes.

Serves: 4 to 6
Serving Suggestions: This soup is hearty enough to be served as a luncheon entrée accompanied by a salad and crusty bread or rolls.
Note: This recipe requires advance preparation.
HEAT SCALE: 3

Tomato Chutney

(INDIA)

Chutneys are the Indian counterparts of the hot chile salsas of the Western Hemisphere and are usually served to accompany meats, fish, and fowl.

6 green chiles, skinned, seeds removed, chopped
1/2 teaspoon powdered ginger
1 1/2 teaspoons paprika
4 large tomatoes, peeled and chopped
1 medium onion, chopped
2 cloves garlic, chopped
1/3 cup red wine vinegar
1/2 cup sugar
1 teaspoon salt

Combine the chiles, tomatoes, onion, and garlic in a saucepan. Bring to a boil and simmer until the tomatoes are soft and broken down—about 30 minutes. Remove and puree until the mixture is a smooth sauce.

Add the remaining ingredients, bring to a boil, reduce the heat, and simmer for an additional 30 minutes. Allow the chutney to set in the refrigerator for 24 hours before serving.

Yield: 2 cups
Note: This recipe requires advance preparation.
HEAT SCALE: 4

Pakistani Lamb

Although this is a very elaborate and time-consuming dish that requires extra preparation, it is well worth it!

3 teaspoons dried santaka chiles
1/2 cup lemon juice
5 cloves garlic, chopped
1 teaspoon cumin seeds
1/2 teaspoon cinnamon
1/8 teaspoon cardamom seeds
1 teaspoon turmeric
1/2 teaspoon ground cloves
1/4 teaspoon salt
4-pound leg of lamb, trimmed of fat and membrane
1 cup plain yoghurt
1 cup blanched almonds
1/2 cup raisins
1/4 cup honey
1 cup water
Salt to taste

Combine the first 9 ingredients in a blender and puree until it is a smooth paste. Cut slits in the leg of lamb about ³/₄ of an inch apart and 2 inches deep. Rub the paste into the slits and over the rest of the leg and let sit, at room temperature, for an hour.

Puree the yoghurt, almonds, and raisins in a blender until smooth. Place the lamb in a casserole, cover with the yoghurt mixture, and then pour the honey over the top. Cover tightly and marinate 12 hours or more in the refrigerator.

Add the water and salt to the casserole dish and bake the lamb at 350°F for 1¹/₂ hours, then reduce heat to 325°F and bake 45 minutes or until done.

Serves: 6 to 8

Serving Suggestions: Because of the multitude of spices in this recipe, serve the lamb with a plain vegetable and green salad.

Note: This recipe requires advance preparation.

HEAT SCALE: 3

Lamb Curry

(INDIA)

One of the major ingredients of curry is ground cayenne or santaka chiles, which are added in varying amounts for heat intensity. This is a basic, easy to prepare curry that can be dressed up with a wide assortment of condiments.

12 tablespoons curry powder (p. 19)
1 pound lamb, diced
4 tablespoons oil
1 cup onion, chopped
2 cups lamb or beef stock
2 tablespoons flour mixed with 2 tablespoons water

Brown the lamb in the oil. Add the onion and sauté until soft. Add the curry powder and heat, stirring constantly.

Add the stock and simmer until the meat is very tender. Remove the lamb, reserving the liquid. Slowly pour in the flour mixture, bring to a boil, and stir until thickened. Add the lamb and simmer over a low flame until hot.

Serves: 4

Serving Suggestions: Serve the curried lamb on a bed of rice with your combination of the following condiments: chutney, peanuts, raisins, shredded coconut, chopped onions, chopped hard-cooked eggs, chopped apples, chopped bananas, chopped tomatoes.

Variations: For a hotter curry, add cayenne or crushed santakas. Substitute chicken for the lamb.

HEAT SCALE: 5

Beef Curry

(PAKISTAN)

Beef is served only in northern India and countries like Pakistan where the Hindu influence is tempered by Muslims and Christians.

4 dried santaka chiles, crushed
1 tablespoon fresh ginger, peeled and minced
1 small onion, chopped
2 teaspoons coriander seeds
1 teaspoon ground cloves
2 cardamom seeds
2 cups water
2 cloves garlic, minced
4 tablespoons oil
2 pounds beef, cut in 1-inch cubes
1/2 cup plain yoghurt
1/4 teaspoon ground nutmeg

Puree the onion, coriander, cloves, cardamom, and 1/4 cup of the water in a blender until smooth.

Sauté the ginger, garlic, chiles, and spice mixture in the oil for 2 minutes. Add the beef and fry until browned. Add the rest of the water and simmer covered until meat is very tender, about an hour.

Add the yoghurt and nutmeg and stir until well mixed. Simmer for 5 minutes or until the mixture is heated.

Serves: 4 to 6
HEAT SCALE: 6

Tandoori Chicken

(INDIA)

This is a barbecue favorite from northern India, where the restrictions on meat consumption are not so strict as in the rest of the country. A *tandoor* is a deep clay oven; *tandoori* refers to chicken that is marinated in a spiced yoghurt and then broiled.

3 teaspoons chile powder
3 teaspoons fresh ginger, peeled and minced
2 cloves garlic, minced
4 tablespoons plain yoghurt
4 chicken breasts
3 teaspoons toasted cumin seeds, crushed
2 tablespoons oil

Combine the ginger, garlic, and yoghurt and rub the mixture into the chicken breasts. Marinate for 24 hours in the refrigerator.

Mix the chile powder, cumin, and oil together. Pour this mixture over the chicken and grill or charcoal broil until the chicken is done.

Serves: 4
Serving Suggestion: This barbecue is enhanced by a fresh fruit salad.
Note: This recipe requires advance preparation.
HEAT SCALE: 3

Spiced Chicken

(INDIA)

This recipe is typical of the Indian philosophy of cooking with curry. The skin is removed from the chicken, then the spice paste is rubbed in so the heat will penetrate into the flesh.

4–5 red chiles, whole
2 teaspoons fresh ginger, peeled and minced
1 3-pound chicken, cut into serving pieces
1 large onion, chopped
1/2 cup oil
3 tablespoons raw peanuts
4 cloves
2 cardamom seeds
2 teaspoons coriander seeds
4 cloves garlic, minced
1/4 cup plain yoghurt

Remove the skin from the chicken and trim off any excessive fat.

Sauté the onion in 2 tablespoons of the oil until browned. Remove and drain. Grind the chiles, peanuts, cloves, cardamom, and coriander seeds together. Combine this powder with the ginger, garlic, and onion. Puree the mixture until smooth. Stir in the yoghurt. Rub the yoghurt mixture over the chicken and marinate in the refrigerator for 12 hours.

Heat the remaining oil and fry the chicken for 15 minutes on each side. Reduce the heat, cover, and simmer for 45 minutes or until the chicken is tender. Uncover and cook for an additional 10 minutes or until the chicken parts are lightly browned.

Serves: 4
Note: This recipe requires advance preparation.
HEAT SCALE: 4

Shrimp Vindaloo

(INDIA)

Vindaloo describes a style of cooking whereby the main ingredient (shrimp, chicken, or lamb) is marinated for 12 to 24 hours in a vinegar-based sauce with chile and other spices. The marinated meat is then cooked in the marinade.

3 santaka chiles, crumbled
3 teaspoons fresh ginger, peeled and chopped
1 medium onion, chopped
4 cloves garlic, chopped
1 teaspoon ground cumin
2 teaspoons ground turmeric
2 tablespoons oil
1/2 cup cider vinegar
1 pound raw shrimp, peeled and deveined
4 tablespoons butter

Combine the first 8 ingredients and puree in a blender until smooth. Place this sauce in a glass or ceramic bowl, add the shrimp, and toss until well coated. Cover and marinate in the refrigerator for 24 hours.

Sauté the shrimp and marinade in the butter until done.

Serves: 4
Note: This recipe requires advance preparation.
HEAT SCALE: 6

Fish in Yoghurt Sauce

(INDIA)

It is important to note that in this recipe the fish should not be overcooked, as it will disintegrate and be lost in the sauce.

5 fresh green chiles, skinned, seeds removed, chopped fine
3 teaspoons fresh ginger, peeled and chopped
4 white fish fillets, skin removed
Flour for dredging
6 tablespoons oil
1 small onion, chopped
¼ teaspoon each ground turmeric, cinnamon, cloves
1 cup plain yoghurt
Salt to taste

Dredge the fillets in the flour and fry in 4 tablespoons of the oil until browned on both sides. Remove and drain.

Add the additional 2 tablespoons of oil to the pan and sauté the onion until browned. Add the turmeric, cinnamon, and cloves and stir-fry for 2 minutes. Remove, add the yoghurt, and puree in a blender until a smooth sauce. Salt to taste.

Return the sauce to the heat and simmer for 10 minutes. Carefully slip the fillets in the sauce so that they don't fall apart. Cover and simmer only long enough to heat the fish, about 3 to 4 minutes. Sprinkle the chopped chiles on top and serve.

Serves: 4
Serving Suggestions: Serve with rice.
HEAT SCALE: 4

Scrambled Eggs with Ginger

(INDIA)

This breakfast dish will open anyone's eyes.

4 green chiles, skinned, seeds removed, chopped fine
1 teaspoon fresh ginger, peeled and chopped fine
4 tablespoons onions, chopped fine
2 tablespoons butter
6 eggs
1/4 cup milk
Salt and pepper to taste

Sauté the onion and ginger in the butter until the onion is soft. Beat the eggs, milk, salt, and pepper together and pour into the skillet with the onions and ginger. Sprinkle the chiles on top and scramble over a low heat until the eggs are done.

Serves: 4
Serving Suggestions: For breakfast, serve with croissants and fresh melon.
HEAT SCALE: 4

Egg Curry
(INDIA)

This English adaptation of an Indian egg curry makes a good luncheon or brunch entrée.

2 tablespoons curry powder (p. 19)
1 cup onion, finely chopped
2 tablespoons butter
1 tablespoon flour
1 cup milk
8 hard-cooked eggs, chopped
4 toasted English muffins
Fresh cilantro or parsley, chopped

Sauté the onion in the butter until soft. Stir in the curry and flour and heat for an additional 2 minutes. Slowly add the milk, stirring constantly until the sauce thickens. Add the chopped eggs and heat thoroughly. Pour over the muffins, garnish with the cilantro or parsley, and serve.

Serves: 4
Serving Suggestions: Serve with asparagus and fresh fruit compote.
HEAT SCALE: 2

Saffron Rice

(SRI LANKA)

Rice dishes in this form, commonly called pilafs, appear all over the world. This is an exotic version from the country formerly called Ceylon, which has one of the most fiery cuisines in the world.

1/2 cup green chile, skinned, seeds removed, chopped fine
2 teaspoons fresh ginger, peeled and chopped fine
1 teaspoon black mustard seeds
3 1/4 cups water
1/4 teaspoon saffron
1 cup long-grain rice, rinsed well
Salt to taste
2 tablespoons butter
2 ounces unsalted cashew nuts
4 whole cloves
1/2 cup lime juice

Pour 1/4 cup boiling water over the saffron and let soak for 10 minutes.

Cook the rice in 2 cups salted water for 10 minutes, then drain.

Heat the butter until very hot, add the ginger, mustard seeds, cashews, and cloves and fry the mixture, stirring constantly, until the seeds begin to burst. Add the chile, lime juice, rice, and the remaining cup of boiling water and stir well. Pour the saffron water over the mixture and bring to a boil, stirring once. Cover the pan tightly and bake at 350°F for 20 minutes or until the liquid has been absorbed and the rice is tender. Fluff with a fork before serving.

Serves: 4 to 6
HEAT SCALE: 8

Nepalese Boiled Potatoes

Like hamburgers in the United States or pasta in Italy, these "hot" potatoes can be found everywhere in Nepal.

2 tablespoons crushed red chile
½ teaspoon dry mustard powder
1 teaspoon lemon juice
2 tablespoons oil (peanut is preferred)
3 potatoes, boiled and cut in 1-inch cubes

Thoroughly mix the mustard, lemon juice, and oil. Pour the mixture over the hot potatoes. Toss gently to coat all the pieces. Sprinkle the red chile over the potatoes and serve.

Serves: 4
Serving Suggestions: Serve with plain meats and vegetables—these potatoes can be very pungent.
HEAT SCALE: 6

Curried Cauliflower

(INDIA)

Cauliflower is one of the most common vegetables used in Indian cooking. Potatoes may be substituted in this recipe.

4 green chiles, skinned, seeds removed, chopped fine
1/2 teaspoon mustard seeds
1 tablespoon fresh ginger, peeled and chopped fine
2 tablespoons oil
1/4 teaspoon cumin seeds
3/4 cup onion, chopped fine
1/2 teaspoon turmeric
1 head cauliflower, divided into flowerets
2 tomatoes, peeled and chopped
1/2 teaspoon sugar

Heat the oil until very hot and add the mustard seeds, ginger, cumin seeds, and onion. Cook for 2 minutes, stirring constantly. Add the turmeric and continue cooking for an additional 5 minutes. Add the cauliflower and stir until the flowerets are coated with the mixture. Add the remaining ingredients, reduce the heat, and cook until the cauliflower is tender but firm.

Serves: 6
HEAT SCALE: 4

Spicy Peas

(INDIA)

This dish is excellent as a pungent surprise when served as a side dish with a nonspicy meat entrée such as roast beef or pork.

3 dried santaka red chiles
1/2 teaspoon fresh ginger, peeled and minced
1/2 teaspoon cumin seeds
1 tablespoon oil
1/4 teaspoon powdered turmeric
1 pound fresh or frozen peas
1/4 cup water

Toast the cumin seeds in the hot oil for 1 minute. Add the chiles, ginger, and turmeric and sauté for an additional 2 minutes. Stir in the peas, add the water, cover, and simmer until the peas are done.

Serves: 4
HEAT SCALE: 6

11
Southeast Asia and the Pacific

Hot foods are quite prevalent in this area because of the widespread use and cultivation of the smallest and hottest chiles. Burma, Malaysia, Indonesia, and the Philippines seem to enjoy the hottest cuisines, and we have chosen representative dishes from those countries. Other hot ingredients commonly used in food preparation are ginger and curries.

And interesting combination of foods occurs frequently in dishes from the Pacific Islands: chiles and coconut. The coconut preparations are "milk" and "cream" made from the juice and pulp of that huge tropical seed. Since they are so prevalent, we've included those recipes first.

Coconut Milk and Cream

(PACIFIC ISLANDS)

Both of these sauces can be made from either fresh or vacuum-packed flaked coconut.

COCONUT MILK

From fresh coconut: Grate the coconut meat and add 2 cups hot water for every cup of meat. Soak for 30 minutes and squeeze through cheesecloth to extract the liquid.

171

From flaked coconut: Add 2 cups hot milk to each cup flaked coconut. Soak for 30 minutes and squeeze through cheesecloth to extract the liquid.

COCONUT CREAM

From fresh coconut: Add 1 cup hot water to 2 cups grated coconut meat. Let stand for 30 minutes and squeeze through cheesecloth to extract the liquid.

From flaked coconut: Slowly add 1 cup coconut to 1 cup hot heavy cream, taking care that the cream doesn't curdle. Let stand for 30 minutes, then squeeze through cheesecloth.

Note: When cooking with either coconut milk or cream, heat slowly to prevent curdling.

Curried Beef Crescents

(THAILAND)

These spicy beef crescents are similar to the empanaditas of Latin America.

6 green chiles, skinned, seeds removed, chopped
1 tablespoon fresh ginger, peeled and minced
1 small onion, chopped fine
2 cloves garlic, chopped fine
3 tablespoons butter
1 pound ground beef
1/2 teaspoon ground cumin
1/2 teaspoon ground coriander
1/2 teaspoon turmeric
2 tablespoons lime juice
Salt

Sauté the onion and garlic in the butter until soft but not brown. Add the chiles and ginger and simmer for 5 minutes. Brown the beef in the mixture, stirring constantly. When the meat is brown, add the remaining ingredients. Remove from the heat.

PASTRY
1²/₃ cup lard or shortening
2¹/₂ cups flour
1 cup water
¹/₂ teaspoon salt

Cut the shortening into the flour with a pastry blender or two forks until the mixture is the consistency of coarse meal. Add the salt and water and mix until the dough is firm. Roll the dough out until ¹/₈ inch thick and then cut in circles 3 inches in diameter.

TO ASSEMBLE
Place a teaspoon of the beef mixture in the center of each circle, moisten the edges with water, and fold the dough over, pressing the edges to seal and pull the two ends toward the center to form a crescent.

Place on an ungreased baking sheet and bake at 375°F for 25 minutes or until the crusts are golden brown.

Yield: 2 to 3 dozen
Serving Suggestions: In Thailand these crescents are served as an appetizer or hors d'oeuvre.
Variation: Commercial wonton skins may be substituted for the pastry. Fill with the meat and deep-fry.
HEAT SCALE: 4

Beef Saté

(INDONESIA)

These highly seasoned kabobs are made from all sorts of meats, fish, and spicy pastes. They can be large or small and served as an entrée or appetizer. In Indonesia, these satés are most often eaten at roadside stands.

5 green chiles, skinned, seeds removed, chopped
1 1/2-inch piece fresh ginger, peeled and chopped
1 medium onion, chopped
2 cloves garlic, chopped
2 tablespoons grated lemon rind
1 tablespoon dark soy sauce
3 teaspoons coriander
1 teaspoon turmeric
1/3 cup water
1/4 cup peanut oil
1 cup coconut cream (see p. 171)
1 1/2 pounds bottom round of beef, cut in 2-inch cubes

The first 9 ingredients constitute the spicy paste. Pureé them in a blender until smooth.

Heat the oil and sauté the paste for 4 minutes, stirring constantly. Add the coconut cream and slowly bring to a boil, stirring constantly. Add the meat, reduce the heat, and simmer until the meat is tender, about 30 minutes.

While the meat is cooking, soak wooden skewers in water to prevent them from burning during grilling. Thread the meat on the wooden skewers. Grill the satés over charcoal, basting frequently with the sauce until crisp, about 5 to 10 minutes.

Yield: 6 to 8
Serving Suggestions: Serve the kabobs with sauce on the side. They are perfect as an appetizer for a barbecue, or serve with boiled rice and a green vegetable such as snow pea pods.
HEAT SCALE: 4

Vietnamese Spicy Shrimp Pork Salad

Never tell a soul, but leftover pork roast is now a gourmet specialty.

3 teaspoons ground red chiles
2 cloves garlic, minced
1/4 teaspoon ground coriander seeds
2 tablespoons vinegar
2 tablespoons lemon juice
1 teaspoon sugar
Salt and pepper
1 pound shrimp, cooked and diced
1 cup pork, cooked and diced
1 cup cooked thin noodles

Combine the chile, garlic, coriander, vinegar, lemon juice, sugar, salt, and pepper in a bowl. Add the shrimp and pork and toss lightly until well coated. Allow to marinate for 1 hour before serving.

Add the marinated meats to the noodles, toss, and serve.

Serves: 4 to 6
HEAT SCALE: 2

Indonesian Chicken Soup

Basic chicken soup can be greatly altered by changing the garnishes and adding ingredients such as cooked shrimp and hard-cooked eggs.

7 dried chile piquins, crushed, or 3 dried santakas, crumbled
2 inches fresh ginger, peeled and chopped
3-pound chicken, cut up
2 large onions, sliced
1 quart water
2 tablespoons peanut oil
1 teaspoon turmeric
2 teaspoons ground coriander
1/2 teaspoon ground nutmeg
1 cup vermicelli
4 green onions, chopped (including greens)

Cover the chicken and half the onions with water and bring to a boil. Reduce heat and simmer until the chicken is done, about 1 hour. Remove the chicken; strain and save the broth.

Sauté the remaining onion and ginger in the oil until the onion is soft. Stir in the chiles and spices and sauté for 2 more minutes. Add the mixture to the chicken broth, bring to a boil, then reduce heat and simmer for 20 minutes.

Remove the skin from the chicken, pull the meat from the bones, and chop or shred into bite-size pieces. Add the chicken and the vermicelli to the broth and heat until the vermicelli is soft. Garnish with the onions and serve.

Serves: 4 to 6
HEAT SCALE: 6

Green Curry Paste

(THAILAND)

This is the oriental counterpart to South America's red chile paste (p. 95). It is the hottest of the hot Thailand curries due to the large number of small green chiles used. This paste can be cooled down naturally, by reducing the amount of chile or by adding coconut milk or cream (see p. 171). It will keep a month or more in the refrigerator and though it may look like Italian *pesto*, don't confuse the two in your cooking or you'll be sorry.

10–12 serrano chiles, seeds removed, chopped
1 teaspoon fresh ginger, peeled and chopped
1 teaspoon coriander seeds
1 teaspoon caraway seeds
1/4 teaspoon ground cloves
1 teaspoon ground nutmeg
3 cloves garlic, chopped
2 teaspoons grated lemon rind
2 tablespoons green onions, chopped
1 teaspoon shrimp paste
1/4 cup vegetable oil

Combine all the ingredients in a blender or food processor and puree into a smooth paste.

Yield: about 2/3 cup
Serving Suggestions: Use in sauces and combination en-trées where a heat source is required. Also may be used as a condiment.
HEAT SCALE: 8

Sambal

(INDONESIA)

Sambals are condiments—sauces or relishes with one common ingredients—hot chiles. The other ingredients may be plain or fancy, but the sambals are always hot.

6–8 dried red chiles, crushed
3 cloves garlic, minced
1/4 cup peanut oil
1/2 teaspoon shrimp paste
1/4 cup green onions, chopped
2 tablespoons lime juice

Sauté the garlic and the chiles in the oil for 2 or 3 minutes. Stir the shrimp paste into the chile mixture. Add the onions and lime juice and simmer the mixture until thickened. Cool to room temperature before serving.

Yield: 1/2 cup
Serving Suggestions: Serve as an accompaniment to grilled or broiled meats or as a sauce for dipping sates (p. 174). Use sparingly!
HEAT SCALE: 8

Spiced Curry

(THAILAND)

Thailand is known for hot curries—this is a relatively mild one. The cinnamon and brown sugar provide a hint of sweetness to complement the heat.

3 tablespoons curry powder (p. 19)
2 dried red chiles, whole
2 cloves garlic, minced
1 medium onion, chopped
4 tablespoons oil
2 pounds beef, cubed
2 cups beef broth
1 tablespoon brown sugar
1 teaspoon cinnamon
1 cup sour cream
Chopped peanuts or cashew nuts

Sauté the garlic and onion in the oil until soft. Add the beef and brown. Add the curry powder and heat for 2 minutes. Add the broth, chiles, sugar, and cinnamon. Bring to a boil, cover, and simmer until the beef is tender and there is a cup of liquid left. Remove the chiles.

Slowly stir in the sour cream. Garnish with the nuts and serve.

Serves: 4 to 6
Serving Suggestions: Serve with boiled rice and fruit such as chopped apples, bananas, and raisins. Also good with fruit chutneys.
HEAT SCALE: 3

Burmese Beef

Serve this beef dish over thin noodles with hard-cooked egg slices, shredded coconut, and chopped mangos.

3 teaspoons ground red chile
4 teaspoons fresh ginger, peeled and chopped
1 large onion, chopped
3 cloves garlic, chopped
8 tablespoons oil
2 pounds beef, cut in 1-inch cubes
2 tomatoes, peeled and chopped
1 cup water
2 tablespoons soy sauce

Puree the chile, ginger, onion, and garlic into a paste and mix with 6 tablespoons of the oil. Add the beef and toss until well coated. Marinate the beef in the mixture for 4 hours in the refrigerator.

Brown the meat mixture in the remaining oil. Add the tomatoes, water, and soy sauce. Cover and cook until the meat is tender, about 1 hour.

Serves: 4 to 6
Note: This recipe requires advance preparation.
HEAT SCALE: 2

Singapore Spareribs

The chiles provide the heat and the ginger an interesting pungency in these ribs with an oriental flavor.

4 green chiles, skinned, seeds removed, chopped
2-inch piece fresh ginger, peeled and chopped
2–3 pounds spareribs, cut in 2- or 3-rib serving pieces
4 cloves garlic, whole
2 tablespoons peanut oil
1 cup pineapple chunks
1 bell pepper, seeds removed, sliced
1 cup pineapple juice
2 tablespoons vinegar
2 tablespoons brown sugar
1 tablespoon dry sherry
1 tablespoon dark soy sauce
2 tablespoons cornstarch mixed with 2 tablespoons water

Rub the ribs with the garlic and bake uncovered on a rack in a 350°F oven for 1 hour.

Sauté the chiles in the oil for 2 minutes. Add the pineapple chunks and sauté for 3 more minutes. Add the remaining ingredients except the cornstarch and bring to a boil. Reduce the heat and simmer for 10 minutes.

Remove the ribs from the oven and pour off the fat. Baste the ribs with the sauce and cook an additional hour, basting frequently until the ribs are crisp.

Remove the ribs and place the roasting pan over a medium heat. Add the remaining sauce, bring to a boil, and slowly stir in the cornstarch until the sauce thickens and becomes translucent. Pour the sauce over the ribs and serve.

Serves: 6 to 8
Serving Suggestions: Serve with plain boiled rice and Chinese spinach.
HEAT SCALE: 3

Marinated Pork

(BURMA)

There are many versions of marinated pork in Burma. We have included our favorite and a variation.

3 teaspoons ground red chile
3 teaspoons fresh ginger, peeled and minced
1 medium onion, coarsely chopped
2 tablespoons lime juice
2 tablespoons oil
1 tablespoon light soy sauce
2 tablespoons water
Salt to taste
1–1 1/2 pounds boneless pork, cut in 1-inch cubes

Combine all the ingredients, except the pork, in a blender and puree until smooth. Marinate the pork in the mixture for 3 hours.

Place the pork on skewers and broil over charcoal until the pork is crisp, basting frequently with the marinade.

Serves: 4 to 6
Variation: Substitute 3 tablespoons curry powder for the ginger, and honey for the oil, for a sweeter marinade.
Note: This recipe requires advance preparation.
HEAT SCALE: 3

Sautéed Pork

(CAMBODIA)

For a quick and easy dinner, serve this pork dish with stir-fried rice and vegetables such as snow peas and sprouts.

4 dried santaka chiles, crumbled
2 pounds lean pork, cut in 1-inch cubes
1 cup onion, chopped fine
2 cloves garlic, minced
1 tablespoon oil (peanut preferred)
3 tablespoons light soy sauce
1 cup water
2 tablespoons brown sugar
1 tablespoon vinegar

Sauté the chiles, pork, onion, and garlic in the oil for 10 minutes, stirring constantly. Add the remaining ingredients and simmer, stirring occasionally until the pork is tender.

Serves: 6
HEAT SCALE: 5

Hawaiian Curried Chicken

Hawaii is the crossroads of many cultures and this recipe reflects the variety that can be found in Pacific Island cookery.

2 tablespoons curry powder (p. 19)
2 teaspoons fresh ginger, peeled and minced
1 small onion, chopped
2 tablespoons butter
2 cups coconut milk (p. 171)
2 tablespoons flour mixed with 2 tablespoons water
2 pounds cooked chicken, cut in cubes
¹/₂ cup shredded coconut
¹/₂ cup pineapple chunks

Sauté the ginger and onion in the butter until soft. Add the curry powder and heat for an additional 2 minutes. Slowly add the coconut milk, stirring constantly. Simmer over low heat for 30 minutes, being careful not to let it boil. Remove and strain.

Return the sauce to the heat and slowly stir in the flour and heat until slightly thickened. Add the chicken and simmer for 10 minutes or until the chicken is heated. Top with the coconut and pineapple chunks and serve.

Serves: 4 to 6
HEAT SCALE: 2

Malaysian Chicken

Once again, peanuts crop up in combination with hot chiles.

4 dried red chiles, crumbled
1 large onion, chopped fine
2 cloves garlic, minced
1/4 cup peanut oil
1 tablespoon brown sugar
2- to 3-pound chicken, cut into pieces
4 tablespoons light soy sauce
4 tablespoons wine vinegar
2 tablespoons water

Sauté the chiles, onion, and garlic in the peanut oil until the onion is soft. Add the sugar and sauté until the onion turns brown. Add the chicken and fry until the chicken is uniformly browned.

Combine the remaining ingredients, add to the chicken, cover, and simmer for 15 minutes. Remove the cover and cook over moderate heat for 30 minutes, or until the chicken is tender, basting occasionally with the sauce.

Serves: 4 to 6
HEAT SCALE: 4

Malaysian Spiced Duck

Malaysians are very fond of curry dishes but seldom use a commercial curry powder. Spice pastes are prepared for each individual dish.

3 teaspoons ground dried red chile
2 teaspoons ground ginger
1 teaspoon ground cumin
2 teaspoons ground coriander
1 large onion, chopped fine
2 cloves garlic, minced
1 cup cashew nuts, ground
1 onion, sliced thin and separated into rings
1 cup coconut cream (see p. 171)
Salt
2 cups bread crumbs
3 hard-cooked eggs, chopped
5-pound duck

Puree the ginger, cumin, coriander, chopped onion, garlic, and cashews to make a paste. Reserve 2 tablespoons of the spice paste and combine the rest with the chile, sliced onion, ³/₄ cup of the cocunut cream, and salt. Cook over a low heat for 15 minutes. Add the bread crumbs and eggs. Stuff the duck with the mixture.

Mix the remaining 2 tablespoons of the spice paste with ¹/₄ cup of the coconut cream and rub the outside of the duck with the mixture. Roast the duck in a 350°F oven until tender—about 1¹/₂ to 2 hours, basting frequently with any remaining spice paste and the drippings. Prick the skin of the duck frequently to allow the excess fat to escape.

Serves: 6
HEAT SCALE: 2

Curried Duck

(PHILIPPINES)

Curry is said to remove the fat, gamey taste of duck, as evidenced by this recipe.

2 tablespoons curry powder (p. 19)
2-inch piece of fresh ginger, peeled and minced
1 duck, cut in 2-inch pieces
2 tablespoons oil
2 cups water
2 tablespoons catsup
2 teaspoons light soy sauce
4 green onions, chopped (including greens)

Sauté the duck pieces in the oil until browned. Pour off the fat. Mix the curry powder, ginger, water, catsup, and soy sauce together. Add to the duck and simmer for 45 minutes or until the duck is tender. Garnish with the onions.

Serves: 4 to 6
Serving Suggestions: Serve over rice.
HEAT SCALE: 2

Shrimp in Green Curry Paste

(THAILAND)

The green color is derived from the green chiles used in the paste. This is a relatively easy curry to prepare.

4 tablespoons green curry paste (see p. 177)
1 cup coconut milk (see p. 171)
2 pound raw shrimp, peeled and deveined
2 cups green onions, chopped (including the greens)

Simmer half the coconut milk and the green curry paste for 5 minutes. Add the shrimp, stirring occasionally until the shrimp are cooked. Add the remaining coconut milk and simmer uncovered for an additional 10 minutes. Garnish with the onions.

Serves: 4 to 6
Serving Suggestions: Serve over rice.
Variation: Cooked chicken may be substituted for the shrimp.
HEAT SCALE: 6

Indonesian Shrimp

Coconut milk, ginger, and chiles are a common combination in Indonesian cooking. This shrimp dish could well be a part of a *rijsttafel*, which is an elaborate Sunday brunch lasting for hours.

3 teaspoons ground red chile
1 teaspoon fresh ginger, minced
1 clove garlic, minced
¹/₂ cup onion, minced
2 teaspoons brown sugar
2 teaspoons lemon juice

2 tablespoons oil
1 pound raw shrimp, peeled and deveined
1 cup coconut milk (see p. 171)

Puree the first six ingredients in a blender until a smooth paste. Sauté the paste in oil for 5 minutes, stirring constantly.

Add the shrimp and sauté, stirring constantly, until the shrimp are no longer pink. Slowly add the coconut milk, cover, and simmer for 15 to 20 minutes.

Serves: 2 to 4
HEAT SCALE: 3

Fried Spiced Fish

(THAILAND)

A whole cooked fish is an impressive entrée and this pungent example is no exception.

4 red chiles, seeds removed, crushed
2-inch piece ginger, peeled and chopped
2- to 3-pound red snapper, cleaned but left whole
Cornstarch for dredging
Oil for deep-frying
2 tablespoons peanut oil
2 cloves garlic, minced
1/4 cup wine vinegar
1/4 cup water
2 tablespoons light soy sauce
4 tablespoons brown sugar
1/4 cup green onions, chopped (including greens)
2 tablespoons cornstarch dissolved in 2 tablespoons water

Make 4 or 5 deep incisions in each side of the fish and dredge in the cornstarch. Heat the oil in a large frying pan until very hot.

Gently lower the fish in the oil and fry until browned, about 5 to 10 minutes. Remove and drain.

Sauté the chiles, ginger, and garlic in the peanut oil for 2 to 3 minutes. Add the remaining ingredients, except the cornstarch, and bring to a boil. Reduce heat and simmer for 5 minutes. Slowly stir in the cornstarch until the sauce thickens and turns translucent. Pour the sauce over the fish and serve whole.

Serves: 4 to 6
Serving Suggestions: Accompany with fresh fruit slices or a chutney.
HEAT SCALE: 3

Nasi Goreng
(INDONESIA)

Indonesia's version of fried rice can be made with one or more main ingredients—meat, chicken, or vegetables topped with chopped nuts.

2 1/2 teaspoons dried santaka chiles, crushed
3 teaspoons curry powder (p. 19)
1 cup rice, rinsed well
2 cups chicken broth
3 tablespoons oil (peanut preferred)
3 eggs, lightly beaten
1 large onion, chopped fine
3 cloves garlic, minced
2 cups cooked chicken, cut in slices
1 cup cooked shrimp, diced
4 tablespoons cashews, chopped
2 tablespoons soy sauce

Cook the rice in the chicken broth.

Heat 1 tablespoon of the oil in a pan until hot. Add the eggs and fry for 3 minutes on a side. Remove the omelet and cut into strips.

Sauté the onion and garlic in the rest of the oil until soft, add the chiles and curry powder, and cook an additional 2 minutes. Stir in the rice and sauté until the rice is brown. Add the remaining ingredients and omelet strips and cook over a low heat, stirring occasionally, for 15 minutes or until thoroughly heated.

Serves: 4 to 6
HEAT SCALE: 5

12
The Orient

Every hot ingredient discussed so far in this book appears in oriental cooking, which is indicative of the diversity of cuisines in this part of the world. Horseradish appears in Japan to spice up sushi and sashimi; ginger in various forms is combined with beef and chicken; Szechuan peppercorns make their appearance in the hotter Chinese dishes; mustard is a common ingredient throughout the Orient; and chiles are particularly prevalent in the fiery fare of Hunan and Szechuan provinces of China and in Korea.

With the recent popularity of the hotter Chinese foods comes the myth that Szechuan dishes are too hot to eat. Cooks should remember that the goal is not to obscure taste with heat, but rather to combine heat with subtle flavor. Since one can always make the dish more fiery by simply adding chiles, it is advisable when working with santaka chiles to first add half the chiles required by the recipe, then test for heat and add more as required.

Most of the recipes in this chapter can be cooked with a wok. If you are wok-less, substitute a large stainless steel frying pan with a lid.

Mustard Chicken Shreds

(CHINA)

This dish should be served on individual plates to be eaten as an appetizer (or salad) with chopsticks.

4 teaspoons hot Chinese mustard powder
2 tablespoons wine vinegar
2 tablespoons dark soy sauce
2 tablespoons peanut oil
4 teaspoons sugar
2 teaspoons water
2 cups cooked chicken, cut in thin strips
1 egg, slightly beaten
1/2 cup cornstarch
1 cup oil for frying
2 carrots, grated
4 green onions, including the greens, chopped

Mix the first six ingredients together and set aside. Coat the chicken shreds with egg and then cornstarch. Deep-fry the chicken in the oil until crisp. Remove and drain.

Arrange the chicken on top of the bed of carrots and pour the sauce over the top. Garnish with the green onions and serve.

Serves: 4
HEAT SCALE: 2

Chile Oil

(CHINA)

This oil will keep indefinitely in the refrigerator. It may turn cloudy, but when set at room temperature it will clear. The addition of chile oil will add "fire" to any recipe.

10 dried santaka chiles
2 cups oil (peanut preferred)

Heat the oil until hot, add the peppers, seeds and all, cover, and cook over a low heat until the peppers turn black. Remove from the heat and cool. Cover and let sit at room temperature for 8 hours. Strain through cheesecloth, cover, and refrigerate.

Yield: 2 cups
Serving Suggestions: This oil can be used as a dip or when you want a subtle chile flavor when frying or sautéing—caution, use only a small amount!
Note: This recipe requires advance preparation.
HEAT SCALE: 9

Spicy Chinese Salad

This salad may be served either hot or cold as a separate course between entrées rather than the American way at the beginning of a meal.

4 dried red chiles, broken into pieces
2 carrots, julienne-cut
2 turnips, julienne-cut
Water
1 teaspoon salt

2 cucumbers, julienne-cut
1/2 medium onion, cut into thin wedges and separated
1 clove garlic, minced
2 tablespoons oil
1 tablespoon rice wine vinegar
2 teaspoons sugar

Soak the carrots and turnips in cold water to cover for 15 minutes, drain, and dry. Salt the cucumbers and let sit for 15 minutes. Rinse and dry.

Stir-fry all the ingredients in the oil for 2 minutes. Let the mixture cool to room temperature and chill in the refrigerator for 1 hour before serving.

Serves: 4 to 6
HEAT SCALE: 4

Cucumber Salad

(KOREA)

Cucumbers and chile are a combination that appears in many cuisines throughout the world. This recipe is a good representative salad.

1 1/2 tablespoons crushed red chile
3 cucumbers, sliced thin
Salt
2 cloves garlic, minced
3 tablespoons rice wine vinegar
1 tablespoon sugar
2 tablespoon oil
1 medium onion, sliced thin and separated into rings

Liberally salt the cucumber slices and let stand for 1 hour. Rinse well with cold water and drain.

Mix the chile, garlic, vinegar, sugar, and oil together. Arrange the cucumbers and onion in a bowl and pour the dressing over them. Marinate in the refrigerator for 2 hours before serving.

Serves: 4
Note: This recipe requires advance preparation.
HEAT SCALE: 5

Hot Ginger Spinach Salad

(CHINA)

Summer days in the Szechuan and Hunan provinces can be extremely hot. During such heat, people prefer fresh vegetables and salads over meat dishes.

DRESSING
3 teaspoons crushed red chile
1-inch piece fresh ginger, peeled and minced
2 tablespoons light soy sauce
3 tablespons oil (sesame preferred)
1 teaspoon sugar
¼ teaspoon salt

Heat all the ingredients and keep warm until ready to serve.

SALAD
1 pound spinach, torn into bite-sized pieces
4 green onions, chopped (including greens)

Combine the spinach and onions in a large bowl. Pour the hot dressing over the spinach, toss, and serve immediately.

Serves: 4
HEAT SCALE: 3

Kim Chee
Korean Pickled Cabbage

Kim chee is a national dish in Korea. There are many variations of this fermented "salad"—we have included a milder one.

4–5 fresh green chiles, skinned, seeds removed, chopped fine
2 teaspoons fresh ginger, peeled and grated
1 head Chinese cabbage, coarsely chopped
Salt
6 green onions, chopped (including the greens)
1 clove garlic, minced
Water

Salt the cabbage and let stand for 1 hour. Rinse well with cold water and drain.

Add the remaining ingredients to the cabbage and cover with water. Allow the mixture to pickle in the refrigerator for 2 to 4 days.

To serve, drain off the water and warm to room temperature.

Serves: 6 to 8
Serving Suggestions: Excellent with broiled or grilled meats as a relish.
Note: This recipe requires advance preparation.
HEAT SCALE: 4

Szechuan Spiced Noodles

Noodles in northern China are served like rice in southern China; they are indeed a staple. This dish is prepared in the hot summer when a cool food is a welcome treat.

1 tablespoon chile oil (p. 194)
2 teaspoons ginger, peeled and minced
1/2 teaspoon Szechuan peppercorns, crushed
1 clove garlic, minced
3 tablespoons dark soy sauce
1/4 cup oil (sesame preferred)
3 tablespoons rice vinegar
4 teaspoons sugar
2 tablespoons oil (peanut preferred)
1 pound shrimp, peeled and deveined
2 cups cooked pork, julienne-cut
2 stalks celery, julienne-cut
1 cup green onions, including greens, chopped
1 pound thin egg noodles, cooked

Combine the chile oil, half the ginger, peppercorns, garlic, soy sauce, sesame oil, vinegar, and sugar together in a bowl. Set aside.

Heat the peanut oil and add the rest of the ginger. Stir-fry the shrimp and pork until done, about 10 minutes, and remove. Then stir-fry the celery until slightly soft, remove, and drain.

Place the noodles on a platter, add the celery, and top with the shrimp mixture. Pour the sauce over the top and garnish with the onions.

Serves: 4 to 6
Serving Suggestions: Present this dish as an entrée served with a clear soup.
HEAT SCALE: 4

Korean Short Ribs

The Koreans are quite fond of marinating beef, chicken, or pork in soy-based sauces and then grilling or barbecuing the meat at the table.

4 teaspoons dry hot Chinese mustard
1/2 cup light soy sauce
1/4 cup oil (peanut or sesame preferred)
3 tablespoons white vinegar
2 tablespoons sugar
4 green onions, minced
1 clove garlic, minced
2 pounds short ribs, cut in small sections

Mix all ingredients together, except the ribs. Score the ribs, place in a bowl, and add the marinade, mixing well. Marinate the ribs overnight in the refrigerator.

Broil or grill over charcoal, basting frequently with the sauce until done.

Serves: 4
Serving Suggestions: Good with rice dishes or as an appetizer to an oriental meal with multiple courses.
Note: This recipe requires advance preparation.
HEAT SCALE: 1

Chinese Beef Curry

Compared to its Pakistani counterpart (p. 160), this beef curry dish is less pungent and easier to prepare.

3 tablespoons curry powder (p. 19)
2 teaspoons fresh ginger, peeled and minced
2 tablespoons oil (peanut preferred)
1 clove garlic, minced
1 pound beef, cubed (sirloin or tenderloin preferred)
1 large onion, cut in wedges
1 tablespoon light soy sauce
1 cup beef bouillon
2 tablespoons cornstarch mixed with 2 tablespoons water

Heat the curry powder until hot. Stir in the oil and sauté the ginger and garlic in the mixture. Add the meat and brown. Add the onion and sauté until transparent.

Stir in the soy sauce and bouillon, cover, and bring to a boil. Reduce the heat and simmer until the meat is tender. Slowly stir in the cornstarch mixture and heat until the sauce is thick, stirring constantly.

Serves: 4
Serving Suggestions: Rice, of course, and steamed snow pea pods should accompany this entrée.
HEAT SCALE: 2

Beef with Hot Peppers

(CHINA)

A classic Szechuan dish. Other oriental vegetables such as bamboo shoots and bean sprouts may be added.

2 dried santaka chiles, crumbled
3 green chiles, skinned, seeds removed, cut into strips
4 tablespoons oil (peanut preferred)
1 pound flank steak, cut thinly across the grain
1 tablespoon light soy sauce
1 tablespoon dark soy sauce
2 teaspoons sugar
2 tablespoons rice wine or dry sherry
1/4 pound snow peas
2 carrots, julienne-cut
2 tablespoons cornstarch mixed with 1/4 cup water

Heat the oil in a wok and stir-fry the beef until dry—about 5 to 8 minutes. Remove the meat, and pour off all but 1 tablespoon of the oil. Add the santaka chiles and cook until they start to smoke—about 2 minutes. Remove the chiles.

Combine the soy sauces, sugar, and wine. Return the meat to the wok, add the soy sauce mixture, and cook for 5 minutes. Add the carrots, snow peas, and green chiles and stir-fry for 2 minutes. Slowly stir in the cornstarch and heat, stirring constantly, until thick.

Serves: 4 to 6
HEAT SCALE: 4

Stir-Fried Ginger Beef

(CHINA)

Originating from northern China, this recipe is one of the few beef dishes from a region that serves mostly poultry and pork.

3 teaspoons crushed red chile
2 teaspoons fresh ginger, peeled and shredded
2 tablespoons soy sauce
2 teaspoons sugar
1 tablespoon rice wine or dry sherry
1 pound lean sirloin or tenderloin or flank steak, shredded
4 tablespoons oil
1 cup celery, julienne-cut
1/2 cup bamboo shoots, shredded
1/4 cup beef broth
2 tablespoons cornstarch mixed with 1/4 cup water
1 cup green onions, chopped (including the tops)

Mix together the soy sauce, sugar, and wine. Toss the beef in the mixture and marinate for 1 hour.

Stir-fry the beef in two tablespoons of the oil until browned, then remove and drain. Heat the remaining 2 tablespoons of the oil, add the chile, ginger, celery, and bamboo shoots. Stir-fry for 2 minutes.

Return the beef to the wok, add the broth, and slowly stir in the cornstarch mixture, stirring until the mixture thickens. Add the green onions and serve.

Serves: 4
Note: This recipe requires advance preparation.
HEAT SCALE: 3

Barbecued Hot Lamb

(MONGOLIA)

This recipe combines lamb and chile oil, which is common to central Asia.

4 tablespoons hot chile oil, or combine 2 teaspoons cayenne
    powder and 4 tablespoons oil
1 pound lamb, cut into 1¹/₂-inch cubes
4 tablespoons fresh lemon juice
3 cloves garlic, minced
¹/₄ teaspoon salt

Combine all ingredients in a bowl and marinate for at least 2 hours. Drain the lamb, reserving the marinade for basting. Barbecue the meet on skewers over a hot charcoal fire. Baste and barbecue until done.

Serves: 4
Serving Suggestions: Serve over rice or wheat pilaf.
Note: This recipe requires advance preparation.
HEAT SCALE: 6

Mongolian Fire Pot

A Mongolian fire pot is similar to a beef fondue except that a spicy broth is used to cook the meat instead of hot oil. All the pungency of this dish is found in the dipping sauces. The broth is drunk at the end of the meal. A fondue pot can be substituted for a fire pot.

4 cups beef broth
6 green onions, chopped (including greens)
3 tomatoes, peeled and chopped
1 pound pork or lamb or beef flank steak, sliced against the grain
*   in thin slices (or combine meats)*
1 pound Chinese cabbage, cut in bite-size pieces
1 pound fresh spinach, cut in bite-size pieces
1/4 pound bean curd, cut into bite-size pieces

Combine the broth, green onions, and tomatoes in a pot and bring to a boil. Reduce the heat and simmer for 20 minutes. Transfer to a fondue or fire pot. Meat and vegetables are speared with chopsticks or fondue forks and cooked for a couple of minutes in the broth, then dipped in the following sauces.

CHILE-SOY SAUCE
1/4 cup red chile sauce (see p. 31)
1 1/2 teaspoons chile oil (see p. 194)
1/4 cup soy sauce
1/4 cup rice wine or dry sherry
1/4 cup lemon juice
1/4 cup green onions, chopped

Mix all ingredients together in a pan and heat slowly until hot. Simmer 10 minutes before serving.

Yield: 1 cup
HEAT SCALE: 6

MUSTARD OIL DIP
3 tablespoons dry hot Chinese mustard powder
1 tablespoon sesame oil

Mix the mustard with enough water to make a thin paste, then mix the oil in. Mustard will lose its flavor and strength if prepared too far in advance. It is best to make this dip within a half hour before serving.

Serves: 4
HEAT SCALE: 2

GINGER-SOY DIP
1/4 cup fresh ginger root, peeled and shredded
1/4 cup red wine vinegar
2 tablespoons light soy sauce

Mix ingredients in a serving bowl, cover, and allow to stand at room temperature for at least 10 minutes before serving. This dip will keep for hours at room temperature.

Yield: 1/2 cup
HEAT SCALE: 1

HOT VINEGAR DIP
3 santaka chiles, crumbled
1/2 cup red wine vinegar
1/2 cup dark soy sauce
2 tablespoons peanut oil

Combine the chiles, vinegar, and soy sauce in a serving bowl. Heat the oil until it is quite hot and pour over the mixture.

Yield: 1/2 cup
HEAT SCALE: 6

Chicken with Peppers and Peanuts

(CHINA)

Chicken with peppers is a famous Szechuan dish. We have incorporated peanuts for added texture. The firepower of the dish, which traditionally is very hot, can be reduced by adding fewer chile piquins.

8 chile piquins, dried, whole
1 teaspoon fresh ginger, peeled and minced
2 tablespoons rice wine
3 tablespoons soy sauce
1 chicken, cut into bite-size pieces
3 tablespoons cornstarch
Oil for deep-frying
1/4 cup raw Spanish peanuts
3 tablespoons oil
1 teaspoon sugar
2 tablespoons cornstarch mixed with 1/4 cup water

Mix 1 tablespoon each of the wine and soy sauce. Add the chicken and toss until coated. Coat the chicken with the cornstarch and deep-fry until crisp. Remove and drain.

Sauté the chiles, ginger, and peanuts in 3 tablespoons oil for 2 minutes. Add the fried chicken, remaining wine, soy sauce, and sugar and bring to a boil. Slowly stir in the cornstarch mixture and heat until the sauce thickens.

Serves: 4
Serving Suggestions: The heat of the chiles in this dish complements sweet and sour dishes. Traditionally served over rice.
HEAT SCALE: 7

Sashimi and Sushi

(JAPAN)

As simple as it seems, these two Japanese specialties are not easily prepared. The serving of raw seafood in Japan is regarded as an art, and sushi chefs apprentice for many years to learn the precise techniques of preparation and serving. Sashimi is sliced raw seafood; sushi combines the raw seafood with cooked cold rice. For ease of preparation we have simplified the complicated ritual. The raw seafood suggested can be shrimp, octopus, squid, and the following fish: yellowtail (amberjack), tuna, bonito, salmon.

2 tablespoons powdered wasabi (Japanese horseradish)
4 tablespoons fresh ginger, peeled and sliced very thin
20 pieces sliced raw seafood
1/2 cup soy sauce
1 cup cooked rice of a sticky consistency

White fish may be sliced into small fillets 1 inch by 1½ inches. The shrimp, after peeling and cleaning, may be sliced or served whole, and may be parboiled for 1 minute if desired. Finely slice the tougher meats like squid and octopus.

Reconstitute the wasabi by mixing with a small amount of water. Place equal amounts of soy sauce in two shallow bowls and add the wasabi, adjusting for individual taste as this variety of horseradish is very pungent.

The seafood may be served as sashimi by simply dipping it in the sauce and eating it with your fingers or chopsticks. Between pieces, a portion of fresh ginger is consumed.

To make sushi, form the rice into oblong portions 1½ inches long by ½ inch high. Place the seafood atop the rice, and using your fingers, dip the sushi in the sauce and eat it in one bite. Etiquette for sushi requires use of fingers only (no chopsticks) and no nibbling.

Serves: 2
Serving Suggestions: Serve with green tea and tempura vegetables.
HEAT SCALE: 2

Braised Chinese Fish

The fish in this dish is cooked and served whole, which preserves more of the flavor. In selecting a whole fish, be sure the eyes are clear and bright—the sign of a fresh fish.

3 tablespoons red chile powder
2 teaspoons fresh ginger, minced
4 bean curd cakes, cut in 1-inch squares
2 pounds whole white fish
Salt to taste
6 green onions, sliced (including the greens)
1 clove garlic, minced
2 tablespoons soy sauce
3 tablespoons oil
1 teaspoon sugar
1 cup chicken broth

Cook the bean curd cakes in boiling water for 15 minutes, then drain. Rub salt into the cleaned fish.

Sauté the chile, ginger, onions, garlic, soy sauce, and sugar in the oil for 2 minutes. Place the fish in the pan or wok and brown on both sides. Add the broth, cover, and cook for 15 minutes over a low heat or until the fish flakes with a fork. Add the bean curd and serve.

Serves: 4 to 6
HEAT SCALE: 4

Broiled Lobster

(CHINA)

A sweet and sour dish is a complement to this very fiery recipe. The heat can be tempered by reducing the amount of chile oil, but remember to compensate by adding an equal amount of peanut oil.

¹/₂ cup chile oil (p. 194)
¹/₂ cup rice wine or dry sherry
¹/₂ cup light soy sauce
1-pound lobster, diced
Oil for stir-frying

Combine the chile oil, rice wine, and soy sauce. Add the lobster and toss until well coated and marinate for 2 hours in the refrigerator. Drain.

Stir-fry the lobster in the hot oil until done.

Serves: 4
Variation: Substitute shelled shrimp for the lobster.
Note: This recipe requires advance preparation.
HEAT SCALE: 8

Hunan Shrimp

Once again shellfish is combined with chile and ginger—plus black pepper. The pungency in the shrimp is caused by lengthy marinating, but it is worth the wait.

2 santaka chiles, crumbled, or 4 teaspoons dried red chile powder
2 teaspoons fresh ginger, peeled and minced
1 teaspoon Szechuan peppercorns, ground
¹/4 cup rice wine or dry sherry
1 teaspoon sugar
1 pound shrimp, peeled and deveined
¹/2 cup peanut oil

Combine the first five ingredients in a bowl, add the shrimp, mix well, and marinate overnight in the refrigerator. Drain and reserve the marinade.

Heat the oil until very hot in a wok. Add the shrimp and stir-fry until done, about 10 minutes. Warm the marinade and serve as a sauce for dipping.

Serves: 2 to 4
Note: This recipe requires advance preparation.
HEAT SCALE: 5

Korean Rice

This is the oriental version of a pilaf.

3 teaspoons ground red chile
¹/2 pound pork, diced
2 tablespoons oil
1 cup green onions, chopped
¹/4 pound mushrooms, sliced

1 cup rice, rinsed well
2 tablespoons soy sauce
2 cups chicken broth

Sauté the pork in the oil until no longer pink. Add the chile, onions, and mushrooms and heat until the onions are soft—about 5 minutes. Add the remaining ingredients and bring to a boil. Reduce the heat, cover, and simmer for 20 minutes or until the rice is done.

Serves: 6
HEAT SCALE: 3

Spicy Stir-Fried Vegetables

This is a simple vegetable dish from northern China that combines both ginger and chiles. Other vegetables or a combination of vegetables can be used with the basic recipe.

4 dried red chiles, torn into pieces
¹/2-inch piece fresh ginger, peeled and shredded
¹/4 cup oil
¹/2 head broccoli, broken into flowerets
¹/2 head cauliflower, broken into flowerets
³/4 cup water
1 tablespoon cornstarch mixed with ¹/4 cup water

Heat the oil and stir-fry the chiles and ginger for 10 seconds. Add the vegetables and stir-fry for 2 to 3 more minutes. Add the water, bring to a boil, cover, and cook until the vegetables are done but still crisp (5 to 8 minutes). Stir in the cornstarch mixture and continue stirring until the sauce is thick and clear.

Serves: 4 to 6
Variations: Cashews or peanuts can be added for texture.
HEAT SCALE: 3

13
American Innovations

Despite that fact that chile peppers are native to nearby Mexico, all the hot ingredients and most of the recipes we've seen so far have been imported into the United States. However, it is not necessary for American cooks to be dependent upon foreign foods for a measure of heat in their meals. The fiery cuisine has now been extended into more traditional American recipes, and the results are delightful.

We have included a few innovative hot food recipes from the United States to demonstrate the ongoing spread of spicy ingredients. Cooks are encouraged to experiment with variations of their own so that the fiery cuisine will spread even further.

Pungent Vegetable Soup

What a surprise for your luncheon guests! It is proper form to warn them before serving that this soup is a bit different from what they might expect.

4 teaspoons crushed red chile
1 small onion, diced
$^{1}/_{2}$ cup carrots, diced
$^{1}/_{2}$ cup celery, diced

¹/4 cup butter
¹/2 cup diced potatoes
¹/2 cup whole-kernel corn
4 tomatoes, peeled and chopped
4 cups chicken broth
1 tablespoon parsley, chopped
Salt and pepper

Sauté the onion, carrots, and celery in the butter for 10 minutes. Add the potatoes and sauté for an additional 5 minutes.

Add the remaining ingredients and bring to a boil. Immediately reduce the heat and simmer for 45 minutes to an hour or until the vegetables are done and the soup is thick.

Serves: 4
HEAT SCALE: 3

Pizza, New Mexico Style

Innocently resembling a normal pizza, this seemingly innocuous favorite will get immediate attention with the first bite.

SAUCE
3 teaspoons ground red chile
2 cloves garlic, minced
1 large onion, chopped
2 tablespoons oil
1 8-ounce can tomato sauce
1 tablespoon dried oregano
1 teaspoon sugar
Salt and pepper

Sauté the onion and garlic in the oil until soft. Add the remaining ingredients, bring to a boil and then reduce the heat and simmer until thick, about 2 hours. Remove and puree in a blender until smooth.

CRUST
3 cups flour (bread flour preferred)
1 package yeast dissolved in 1 cup hot water
2 tablespoons oil
1 teaspoon salt
Freshly ground black pepper

Combine all the ingredients and knead the dough for 5 to 10 minutes until it is smooth and elastic. Cover and let rise for 2 hours or until doubled in size.

Punch down and stretch the dough until it fits a pizza pan. Let sit for 20 minutes.

TO ASSEMBLE
1/2 cup green chile strips
1 cup chopped onion
1/2 cup chopped mushrooms
1/2 cup black olives, sliced
1 cup cooked chorizo, crumbled
1/2 cup grated mozzarella cheese
1/2 cup grated provolone cheese
1/2 cup grated Parmesan cheese
Olive oil

Spread the sauce over the dough. Arrange the chile, onion, mushrooms, olives, and chorizo on top of the sauce. Top with the grated cheeses. Sprinkle olive oil on top. Bake at 400°F for 25 minutes or until the crust is browned.

Serves: 2–4
Note: This recipe requires advance preparation.
HEAT SCALE: 4

Steak à la Dave

The addition of the chile and cheese creates perhaps the all-time perfect steak.

1 cup green chile, skinned, seeds removed, chopped
2 teaspoons freshly ground black pepper
4 teaspoons lemon juice
2 large 2-inch thick steaks, sirloin or filets preferred
2 teaspoons fresh garlic, minced
1 cup cheddar cheese, grated

Sprinkle the lemon juice over each side of steak. Then sprinkle the garlic and black pepper over each side of each steak and pound them gently into the meat. Let the steaks sit at room temperature for at least an hour.

Grill the steaks over a fire of charcoal and mesquite wood. About 6 or 7 minutes before they are done, spread the green chile over each steak and then the cheese. Serve just when the cheese has melted.

Serves: 4
Serving Suggestions: Why not a baked potato and green salad?
HEAT SCALE: 5

Turkey with Chile Stuffing

By adding chile to a traditional corn bread stuffing, a hotter Thanksgiving is in the offing.

1 cup green chile, seeds removed, chopped
¼ pound butter
1 large onion, chopped
1 cup chopped celery (optional)
6 cups corn bread, coarsely crumbled
1 cup whole pine nuts, or chopped walnuts
2 teaspoons thyme
1 + cups chicken broth
10- to 12-pound turkey

Melt the butter in a saucepan and sauté the onion until soft. Combine the onion, chile, celery, corn bread, nuts, and thyme in a bowl and mix thoroughly. Add enough broth to thoroughly moisten, but not saturate, the mixture.

Stuff the turkey cavity and sew shut. Roast at 350°F for 25 minutes per pound. Baste the bird every 15 minutes with melted butter and pan juices.

Serves: 6 to 8
Serving Suggestions: Serve with mashed potatoes, gravy, and squash.
HEAT SCALE: 3

Ginger-Fried Chicken

A traditional Southern favorite, cleverly disguised.

6 *teaspoons ground ginger*
1 *cup flour*
4 *chicken breasts*
Milk
Salt and pepper
¹/₃ cup butter
²/₃ cup oil

Mix together the flour and most of the ginger. Dip the chicken in the milk and let the pieces drain. Lightly sprinkle the chicken with ground ginger, salt, and pepper. Coat the chicken with the seasoned flour.

Brown the chicken quickly in the oil and butter. Cover the pan and cook for 20 minutes. Remove the cover and cook until brown and tender, about 20 more minutes.

Serves: 4
Serving Suggestions: Make a cream gravy and serve with mashed potatoes and green beans.
HEAT SCALE: 1

Chile Corn Bread

A quick and easy spicy bread that goes very well with soups and stews.

3 green chiles, skinned, seeds removed, chopped
1 1/2 cups creamed corn
1 1/2 cups cornmeal
1/3 cup melted shortening
2 eggs, slightly beaten
1/4 cup milk
1 teaspoon baking powder
1/2 teaspoon soda
1 teaspoon sugar (optional)
1 teaspoon salt
1 1/2 cups cheddar cheese, grated

Combine all the ingredients except the chiles and cheese. Pour half the mixture into a greased 9" by 9" baking pan. Sprinkle half the cheese and chiles on top. Add the remaining batter and top with the rest of the cheese and chiles. Bake in a 400°F oven for 45 minutes. Cool slightly before serving.

Serves: 6
HEAT SCALE: 3

Index